SIXTH EDITION

Supplemental Exercises for *Real Writing* and *Real Writing with Readings*

SIXTH EDITION

Supplemental Exercises for *Real Writing* and *Real Writing with Readings*

Susan Anker

Eddye S. Gallagher
Tarrant County College

BEDFORD/ST. MARTIN'S

Boston ♦ New York

Manufactured in the United States of America.

8 7 6 5 4 3
f e d c b a

For information, write: Bedford/St. Martin's 75 Arlington Street, Boston, MA 02116
(617-399-4000)

ISBN 978-1-4576-2431-5

Preface for Instructors

This booklet supplements the exercises in *Real Writing* with 100 exercise sets covering all the topics in the Editing chapters (Chapters 19–38) and with additional exercises on integrating and citing sources (to accompany Chapter 18, "Writing the Research Essay").

Each editing exercise begins with a corrected (or completed) example to help students get started, and most sets are on a single, engaging topic to keep students interested and to help them view editing holistically—not as an isolated activity. Answers to all the exercises appear at the end of the booklet so students can check their own work.

More exercise and test materials are available to *Real Writing* users in the following supplements:

- *Additional Resources for Real Writing,* which includes review tests and many other supplemental materials.

- *Exercise Central,* an online exercise bank with thousands of items (**bedfordstmartins.com/exercisecentral**). Exercises written specifically for *Real Writing* are available at **bedfordstmartins .com/realwriting**.

If you would like more information about these materials or about the complete supplements package for *Real Writing,* please visit **bedfordstmartins.com/realwriting/catalog**, contact your local Bedford/St. Martin's representative, or e-mail sales support (**sales_support@bfwpub.com**). If there are additional resources that you would find helpful in your courses, or if you have student papers to submit for possible inclusion as models and readings in future editions, please let us know by writing to us at *Real Writing,* Bedford/St. Martin's, 75 Arlington Street, Boston, MA 02116.

Thank you.
Susan Anker
Eddye S. Gallagher

Contents

Introduction for Students

This booklet helps you practice the editing and research skills covered in *Real Writing*. Each editing exercise begins with a corrected (or completed) example to help you get started, and answers to all the exercises appear at the end of the booklet so you can check your own work.

Your instructor may assign some of these exercises, or you may choose to do them on your own to get more practice. Especially if you are working on your own, we recommend that you read the relevant chapters (or chapter sections) in *Real Writing* before completing the exercises in this booklet. (Your instructor may want you to do the exercises in the book as well.)

After you have completed the exercises in this booklet, you can check your work in the answer key. If, after doing the exercises, you find that you need more practice in certain areas, consider visiting *Exercise Central* at **bedfordstmartins.com/exercisecentral**. There you will find additional practices on every grammar issue covered in *Real Writing*. *Exercise Central* will give you instant feedback for each item you complete.

Supplemental Exercises for Chapter 18 ("Writing the Research Essay")

18-1: Integrating and Citing Sources within Your Paper

When integrating information that you have gathered from other sources, you may want to use direct quotes, indirect quotes, summaries, and paraphrases. (Making reference in your paper to other people's words and ideas can be a good way to help support your thesis, connect your ideas to a larger conversation, or present a counter view, which you then discuss.) When using these words or ideas from other sources, you will need to make sure that you do not commit plagiarism—using material from an outside source without properly giving credit to the source.

Using the following passage, write on separate paper or your computer a one-sentence summary of the entire passage, a paraphrase of the part of the passage that is in bold type, and a direct quote that could be used in a research essay about the effects of music on the brain. (Be sure to introduce the quote with a signal phrase.) At the end of your summary, paraphrase, or quote, include a parenthetical reference to the original source.

ORIGINAL SOURCE

Music has charms to soothe a savage breast, but scientists are finding that it works those charms through the brain. At a recent conference of the New York Academy of Sciences, [Sandra] Trehub and dozens of other scientists interspersed their PET scans and MRIs with snatches of Celine Dion and Stravinsky as they reported on the biological foundations of music. Several lines of evidence suggest that the human brain is wired for music, and that some forms of intelligence are enhanced by music. **Perhaps the most striking hint that the brain holds a special place in its gray matter for music is that people can typically remember scores of tunes, and recognize hundreds more. But we can recall only snatches of a few prose passages ("Four score and seven years ago . . .").** Also, music affects the mind in powerful ways: it not only incites passion, belligerence, serenity or fear, but does so even in people who do not know from experience, for instance, that a particular crescendo means the killer is about to pop out on the movie screen. All in all, says psychologist Isabelle Peretz of the University of Montreal, "the brain seems to be specialized for music."

—Sharon Begley, "Music on the Mind," *Newsweek*, July 24, 2000, p. 51

18-2: Integrating and Citing Sources within Your Paper

When integrating information that you have gathered from other sources, you may want to use direct quotes, indirect quotes, summaries, and paraphrases. (Making reference in your paper to other people's words and ideas can be a good way to help support your thesis, connect your ideas to a larger conversation, or present a counter view, which you then discuss.) When using these words or ideas from other sources, you will need to make sure that you do not commit plagiarism—using material from an outside source without properly giving credit to the source.

Using the following passage, write on separate paper or your computer a one-sentence summary of the entire passage, a paraphrase of the part of the passage that is in bold type, and a direct quote that could be used in a research essay about feng shui. (Be sure to introduce the quote with a signal phrase.) At the end of your summary, paraphrase, or quote, include a parenthetical reference to the original source.

ORIGINAL SOURCE

Feng shui, for those who have somehow missed its myriad references in pop culture, means wind and water in Chinese. **The 3,500-year-old system, once used only by China's Emperor, is based on the idea that landscapes, buildings and even whole cities have hidden zones of energy** *(qi),* **which can be manipulated by the shape, size and color of a structure as well as its entrances. A building that allows** *qi* **to flow freely is said to have good feng shui, which brings prosperity and success.**

—Ajay Singh, "Luck Be a Stone Lion," *Time,* July 3, 2000, p. 53

18-3: Integrating and Citing Sources within Your Paper

When integrating information that you have gathered from other sources, you may want to use direct quotes, indirect quotes, summaries, and paraphrases. (Making reference in your paper to other people's words and ideas can be a good way to help support your thesis, connect your ideas to a larger conversation, or present a counter view, which you then discuss.) When using these words or ideas from other sources, you will need to make sure that you do not commit plagiarism—using material from an outside source without properly giving credit to the source.

Using the following passage, write on separate paper or your computer a one-sentence summary of the entire passage, a paraphrase of the part of the passage that is in bold type, and a direct quote that could be used in a research essay about racial or ethnic profiling. (Be sure to introduce the quote with a signal phrase.) At the end of your summary, paraphrase, or quote, include a parenthetical reference to the original source.

ORIGINAL SOURCE

According to some agents and prosecutors, snitching is also slowly crippling law enforcement: "Informers are running today's drug investigations, not the agents," says veteran DEA agent Celerino Castillo. "Agents have become so dependent on informers that the agents are at their mercy."

The government's traditional justification for creating criminal snitches—"we-need-to-flip-little-fishes-to-get-to-the-Big-Fish"—is at best an ideal and mostly the remnant of one. Today, the government lets all sorts of criminals, both big and little, trade information to escape punishment for nearly every kind of crime, and often the snitches are more dangerous than the targets.

Snitching thus puts us right through the looking glass: Criminals direct police investigations while avoiding arrest and punishment. Nevertheless, snitching is ever more popular with law enforcement: It is easier to "flip" defendants and turn them into snitches than it is to fight over their cases. For a criminal system that has more cases than it can prosecute, and more defendants than it can incarcerate, snitching has become a convenient case-management tool for an institution that has bitten off more than it can chew.

—Alexandra Natapoff, "Bait and Snitch:
The High Cost of Snitching for Law Enforcement"

The entire essay "Bait and Snitch: The High Cost of Snitching for Law Enforcement" by Alexandra Natapoff is printed in Chapter 47 of *Real Writing with Readings*. This section of the essay appears on page 704–705.

18-4: Integrating and Citing Sources within Your Paper

When integrating information that you have gathered from other sources, you may want to use direct quotes, indirect quotes, summaries, and paraphrases. (Making reference in your paper to other people's words and ideas can be a good way to help support your thesis, connect your ideas to a larger conversation, or present a counter view, which you then discuss.) When using these words or ideas from other sources, you will need to make sure that you do not commit plagiarism—using material from an outside source without properly giving credit to the source.

Using the following passage, write on separate paper or your computer a one-sentence summary of the entire passage, a paraphrase of the part of the passage that is in bold type, and a direct quote that could be used in a research essay about stereotypes and clichés. (Be sure to introduce the quote with a signal phrase.) At the end of your summary, paraphrase, or quote, include a parenthetical reference to the original source.

ORIGINAL SOURCE

Stereotype and cliché serve a purpose as a form of shorthand. **Our need for vast amounts of information in nanoseconds has made the stereotype vital to modern communications.** Unfortunately, it often shuts down original thinking, giving those hungry for truth a candy bar of misinformation instead of a balanced meal. The stereotype explains a situation with just enough truth to seem unquestionable.

All the *isms*—racism, sexism, ageism, et al.—are founded on and fueled by the stereotype and the cliché, which are lies of exaggeration, omission, and ignorance. They are always dangerous. They take a single tree and make it a landscape. They destroy curiosity. They close minds and separate people. The single mother on welfare is assumed to be cheating. A black male could tell you how much of his identity is obliterated daily by stereotypes. Fat people, ugly people, beautiful people, large-breasted women, short men, the mentally ill, and the homeless all could tell you how much more they are like us than we want to think. I once admitted to a group of people that I had a mouth like a truck driver. Much to my surprise, a man stood up and said, "I'm a truck driver, and I never cuss." Needless to say, I was humbled.

—Stephanie Ericsson, "The Ways We Lie"

The entire essay "The Ways We Lie" by Stephanie Ericsson is printed in Chapter 43 of *Real Writing with Readings*. This section of the essay appears on page 664.

18-5: Integrating and Citing Sources within Your Paper

When integrating information that you have gathered from other sources, you may want to use direct quotes, indirect quotes, summaries, and paraphrases. (Making reference in your paper to other people's words and ideas can be a good way to help support your thesis, connect your ideas to a larger conversation, or present a counter view, which you then discuss.) When using these words or ideas from other sources, you will need to make sure that you do not commit plagiarism—using material from an outside source without properly giving credit to the source.

Using the following passage, write on separate paper or your computer a one-sentence summary of the entire passage, a paraphrase of the part of the passage that is in bold type, and a direct quote that could be used in a research essay about willpower. (Be sure to introduce the quote with a signal phrase.) At the end of your summary, paraphrase, or quote, include a parenthetical reference to the original source.

ORIGINAL SOURCE

The researchers confirmed the joys of giving in two separate ways. **First, by surveying a national sample of more than 600 Americans, they found that spending more on gifts and charity correlated with greater happiness, whereas spending more money on oneself did not.** Second, by tracking sixteen workers before and after they received profit-sharing bonuses, the researchers found that the workers who gave more of the money to others ended up happier than the ones who spent more of it on themselves. In fact, how the bonus was spent was a better predictor of happiness than the size of the bonus.

—John Tierney is printed in Chapter 46 of
Real Writing with Readings.

This section of the essay appears on page 692.

Supplemental Exercises for Editing Chapters (*Chapters 19–38*)

Chapter 19: The Basic Sentence: An Overview

19-1: Identifying Parts of Speech

For each of the following sentences, fill in the blank with the correct part of speech of the underlined word. The parts of speech are noun, pronoun, verb, adjective, adverb, preposition, and conjunction.

EXAMPLE

    pronoun   <u>You</u> can learn a lot from family members.

1. _____ Uncle Miguel is my <u>favorite</u> uncle.

2. _____ He <u>takes</u> me to see our town's baseball team play every Friday night.

3. _____ We arrive <u>early</u>, and we try to sit as close to home plate as we can so we can see all the action.

4. _____ <u>We</u> have gotten to know some of the players because we have gone to so many games.

5. _____ <u>At</u> a game one night, a foul ball flew toward us, and I caught it.

6. _____ I keep it on my dresser, <u>and</u> I look at it every night.

7. _____ The best <u>thing</u> about going to the games is spending time with my uncle.

8. _____ <u>He</u> used to play shortstop in high school, and he explains a lot about baseball to me.

9. _____ Last week, he <u>said</u>, "Jenny, you could be a baseball player someday."

10. _____ I would <u>really</u> love to play shortstop, just like Uncle Miguel.

19-2: Identifying Subjects

Underline the subject in each of the following sentences.

EXAMPLE

In the summertime, <u>theaters</u> play lots of movies with expensive special effects.

1. *The Perfect Storm* is a movie starring George Clooney.

2. Before that, it was a best-selling book.

3. The book traces the true story of a fishing boat named the *Andrea Gail.*

4. No one really knows what happened to the *Andrea Gail.*

5. The "perfect storm" was actually three storms that converged at one point.

6. The *Andrea Gail* got caught in the middle of the three storms and never really had a chance.

7. Her sister boat, the *Hannah Boden,* was located six hundred miles away from the *Andrea Gail.*

8. Warning messages about the weather were sent from the *Andrea Gail* to the *Hannah Boden.*

9. The crew of the *Hannah Boden* could prepare the boat for the coming storm.

10. The *Andrea Gail* was able to save her sister boat, but not herself.

19-3: Identifying the Verb

In the following sentences, identify each boldfaced verb as an action verb, a linking verb, or a helping + a main verb.

EXAMPLE

action verb

Of all the winter Olympic sports, I **enjoy** downhill skiing the most.

1. The Winter 2006 Olympics **were held** in Turin, Italy.

2. Turin **is** a popular ski area at the gateway to the Alps.

3. The Olympic park there **provided** a bobsled and luge course and ski jumps for free-style skiers.

4. The Olympics **brought** much attention to this European city.

5. Few Americans **realize** what a beautiful city Turin is.

6. Turin's landscape **makes** it one of the most geologically interesting places in Italy.

7. Castles **surround** the city, and they are popular tourist attractions.

8. Many people **have skied** at Turin's gorgeous resorts over the years.

9. Other parts of Turin **are** industrial; Fiat cars are made there, for instance.

10. Traveling from ancient to modern parts of the city, you **can feel** as though you have traveled through time.

19-4: Identifying Complete Thoughts

State whether each item is an incomplete or complete thought by writing **C** for complete and **I** for incomplete after each sentence.

EXAMPLE

To develop an exercise routine that incorporates jogging.   **I**

1. Though it is hard to believe.

2. Jogging has not always been an American sport.

3. Jogging first became popular in the United States in the late 1970s with the birth of Nike shoes.

4. University of Oregon track coach Bill Bowerman.

5. He experimented with his wife's waffle iron to make the memorable soles of his first running shoes.

6. The shoes with waffle patterns on the bottom made running a more comfortable sport for amateur athletes.

7. Thanks to popular young runners like Steve Prefontaine.

8. Nike shoes became well known almost instantly.

9. Prefontaine's determination and ability to withstand the pain that comes with distance running.

10. Steve Prefontaine inspired many Americans to run in his coach Bill Bowerman's shoes.

Chapter 20: Fragments

20-1: Correcting Fragments That Start with Prepositions

In the following items, correct the fragments by connecting them to the previous or next sentence.

EXAMPLE

> I use my computer for just about everything,/~~F~~rom playing games to paying bills.

1. In 1976, twenty-one-year-old Steven Jobs cofounded Apple Computer, Inc. In his family's garage.

2. In 1984, the team Jobs led created the Apple Macintosh computer. With its user-friendly "point and click" operating system.

3. Yet one year later, Jobs was forced out of his own company. By the board of directors.

4. The Mac revolutionized the computer world. Over the next few years.

5. Apple's rival, the Microsoft Corporation, modeled its Windows operating system. On the Mac.

6. After leaving Apple. Jobs started a computer company called NeXT that developed a cutting-edge new operating system.

7. A British computer programmer created the World Wide Web. On the NeXT system.

8. In 1986, Jobs bought Pixar, a small computer animation studio. From the film director George Lucas.

9. Pixar created the animation. For the 1995 hit movie *Toy Story*.

10. In late 1996, Jobs stunned the computer industry by selling NeXT and its operating system. To his old company, Apple.

20-2: Correcting Fragments That Start with Dependent Words

In the following items, correct the fragments by connecting them to the previous or next sentence.

EXAMPLE

Humans should pay more attention to the natural world/ ͟Because it can teach us so much about ourselves.

1. The zoologist Frans de Waal has spent the past twenty-five years studying. How apes and monkeys behave in captivity.

2. He is a professor of primate behavior at Emory University in Atlanta. Where he is also a researcher at the Yerkes Regional Primate Research Center.

3. While many scientists have emphasized the role of aggression in animal behavior. De Waal stresses the importance of animal kindness and caring.

4. Although animals clearly have rivals. He believes they also have friends.

5. Each group of chimpanzees has a leader. Though De Waal thinks it is the one who makes the best friendships and alliances rather than the one who is the most aggressive.

6. His research on animal relationships has shown that capuchin monkeys will repeatedly find ways to share food. When they are separated from each other by a mesh screen.

7. This sharing is a deliberate choice. Because the monkeys share only with monkeys they like.

8. De Waal believes that the stereotype of the killer-ape is harmful. Since it suggests that human nature is essentially violent and cruel.

9. He argues that morality is an outgrowth of our natural instincts. Which are automatic responses that all people have.

10. If we want to understand what makes us naturally aggressive. We also have to understand what makes us naturally caring.

20-3: Correcting Fragments That Begin with *-ing* Verbs

In the following items, correct the fragments by connecting them to the previous or next sentence.

EXAMPLE

Facing difficult decisions about medical procedures, Patients and their families are often willing to take risks with new technologies.

1. Sharon Bearor was sitting in a doctor's office at Massachusetts General Hospital. Listening to Dr. Allen Lapey explain her son's options.

2. Suffering from cystic fibrosis. Nineteen-year-old Spencer Bean needed two new lungs.

3. However, the long waiting list for an organ donation meant Spencer might die. Waiting for a pair of lungs to become available.

4. Reaching the top of the list. He might also be too sick to go through with the transplant operation.

5. Explaining that there was another option. Dr. Lapey told Spencer and Sharon about an experimental new medical procedure.

6. Doctors could replace a patient's diseased lungs. Using healthy lung tissue from two living relatives.

7. Realizing that Spencer might die without their help. Sharon and her sister Jean decided to donate part of their lungs.

8. Some people are opposed to living-donor transplants. Believing it's unethical to risk harming a healthy person.

9. They also argue that some people might feel pressured to donate organs. Fearing their family's anger if they say no.

10. Ignoring complicated questions of medical ethics. Sharon and Jean simply did what they thought was right.

20-4: Correcting Fragments That Begin with *to* + a Verb

In the following sentences, correct the fragments by connecting them to the previous or next sentence or by adding the missing sentence elements.

EXAMPLE

Most parents will reluctantly admit that they have used television as

a babysitter, To keep their children occupied.

1. Some parents are so fed up with television programming that they want one thing from their families. To kick the TV habit.

2. Producer Linda Ellerbee once threw her TV set out of a second-story window. To get her children's attention when they were watching television.

3. To appease her guilt later in the day. She went out to retrieve the television from her yard. To her amazement, when she plugged it in, it still worked.

4. To study the problem. The Annenberg Public Policy Center has conducted three studies.

5. Parents can use ratings attached to many programs and V-chip technology. To block certain shows they do not want their children to see.

6. Few parents use either method, and most reported they felt powerless. To control their children's viewing habits.

7. According to one researcher, parents have an important role to play. To serve as examples of how much television is acceptable.

8. To give a child his or her own television. Solves many arguments about what to watch, but researchers suggest that this solution means that parents do not know how much television their child is watching.

9. One mother decided to unplug her television one night a week. To show her family that they could survive without television.

10. She reported that everyone struggled, including herself. To keep everyone occupied and busy through the first few weeks. She used all her creative abilities planning activities.

20-5: Correcting Fragments Starting with an Example or Explanation

In the following items, correct the fragments by connecting them to the previous sentence.

EXAMPLE

It can be difficult to make decisions sometimes, Especially when your choice will affect another person.

1. Arthur Caplan is a professor of bioethics. The study of ethical issues relating to medicine, health care, and science.

2. He analyzes complex moral questions. Such as whether society should allow doctor-assisted suicide.

3. Bioethical issues are often featured on TV hospital shows. Like *Grey's Anatomy* and the former hit *Chicago Hope*.

4. Caplan thinks these shows do an okay job of exploring certain bioethical issues. Including the question of whether to give an alcoholic a liver transplant.

5. However, he feels they don't pay enough attention to other kinds of issues. Particularly those relating to money.

6. An episode of *Chicago Hope* was based on one of Caplan's actual cases. A heart transplant in which the doctors didn't know if they had to tell the patient they had dropped the heart on the floor.

7. Caplan believes that it is sometimes ethical to lie. Especially if a life is at stake.

8. He thinks a doctor should lie to help a patient who is being pressured by family members. As in the case of someone who is refusing a blood transfusion for religious reasons.

9. A doctor should also give a phony medical excuse to a family member who doesn't want to donate a live organ. Such as a kidney or lung.

10. Here the moral issue is free choice, not saving a life. As in the example of the blood transfusion.

20-6: Sentence Fragments Review (1)

In the following items, correct the fragments by connecting them to the previous or next sentence.

EXAMPLE

Modern technology has revolutionized our society. In ways that influence our daily lives.

1. Have you ever wondered how a microwave oven cooks food? Without heating the plate.

2. A microwave is an electromagnetic wave. Ranging in frequency from around 1,000 to 300,000 megahertz (MHz).

3. An electromagnetic wave is a vibration. Resulting from the motion of positive and negative electrical charges.

4. There are many different kinds of electromagnetic waves. Such as electric waves, radio waves, infrared radiation, visible light, ultraviolet radiation, X-rays, and gamma rays.

5. Microwaves cook food quickly by making the water molecules in the food vibrate. At a rate of 2,450 million times per second.

6. This vibration absorbs energy from the surrounding electromagnetic field. Causing the food to heat up.

7. The plate and utensils don't get hot. Because their materials don't absorb energy from the magnetic field.

8. Since all the energy is absorbed by the food. Microwave cooking is faster than regular cooking.

9. Many different materials are safe to use in a microwave oven. Like china, glass, plastic, and paper.

10. But you should not use items made out of metal or wood when you microwave. To prevent damage to those items.

20-7: Sentence Fragments Review (2)

In the following items, correct the fragments by connecting them to the previous or next sentence.

EXAMPLE

The best inventors are those who are inspired/ By something simple that no one else sees.

1. Velcro was invented by the Swiss engineer George de Mestral. After he took a walk in the woods with his dog.

2. Arriving back home. He noticed that his socks and his dog were covered with burrs.

3. De Mestral wanted to find out why burrs stick so well. To certain materials. Such as wool and fur.

4. Looking at his socks under the microscope. He discovered that tiny hooks on the ends of the burrs were caught. In the wool's loops.

5. De Mestral figured out a way to copy this natural system. Of hooks and loops.

6. He wove nylon thread into a fabric. Containing densely packed little loops.

7. He cut the loops. On some of the fabric. To make half of each loop a hook.

8. De Mestral called this fabric Velcro. A contraction of the French words *velours* (velvet) and *crochet* (hook).

9. Although Velcro can be peeled apart quite easily. It has extremely high resistance to sideways forces.

10. To prevent equipment, and even astronauts, from floating around. In the space shuttle. Velcro has been used.

Chapter 21: Run-Ons

21-1: Correcting a Run-On or Comma Splice by Adding a Period

In the following items, correct the run-ons and comma splices by adding a period and capitalizing the first letter of the new sentence. Then, indicate whether the item is a run-on or a comma splice by marking **RO** or **CS** in the space provided.

EXAMPLE

Many of the helpful tools we use every day have long histories, the
                                                               T
umbrella was invented in China in the fourth century C.E. ____*CS*____

1. Lead pencils don't really contain any lead they're made out of graphite. _____

2. Lead hasn't been used in pencils since the sixteenth century, it's a good thing because lead is poisonous. _____

3. The ancient Egyptians, Greeks, and Romans used small lead discs to make lines on sheets of papyrus, then they wrote on the papyrus with ink and a brush. _____

4. During the fourteenth century European artists made drawings using rods of lead, zinc, or silver the technique was called silverpoint. _____

5. Wood-encased writing rods were used during the fifteenth century, they were the earliest pencils. _____

6. The modern pencil was developed in 1564 that's when graphite was discovered in Borrowdale, England. _____

7. Graphite is a form of carbon it's greasy and soft with a metallic luster. _____

8. Pencil "lead" is made by mixing graphite with clay and water, then the mixture is fed into a thin cylinder to create sticks. _____

9. More graphite in the mixture makes the pencil softer and blacker, more clay makes it harder and paler. _____

10. The sticks are cut into pencil-sized lengths then they are fired in a kiln at a temperature of about 2,200°F (1,200°C). _____

21-2: Correcting a Run-On by Adding a Semicolon

In the following items, correct the run-ons by adding a semicolon.

EXAMPLE

Many parents wonder how long they should let their babies cry, experts have tried to provide answers.

1. For years, child development specialists have recommended that parents pick up crying babies as soon as possible even 2 minutes of crying can be considered excessive.

2. These experts say that parents should be especially attentive to children under six months of age, tiny babies need reassurance that someone will meet their needs.

3. Letting babies cry too long can raise their blood pressure and levels of stress hormones, it can even interfere with their emotional development, some specialists say.

4. However, some child development experts think that letting a baby cry for a few minutes is not harmful in fact, it can help parents get their children on a consistent sleeping and feeding schedule.

5. For instance, if a baby cries when it's not her usual feeding time, the parents might let her cry and feed her at her regular time, this approach is sometimes known as "controlled crying."

6. In the future, say advocates of this approach, the baby will be more likely to keep to a regular feeding schedule and less likely to cry, others disagree.

7. Opponent of controlled crying say it doesn't guarantee that babies will behave better it might even cause them to feel unloved.

8. These experts often hear criticism that children who are picked up as soon as they cry will become spoiled, their response is essentially "Nonsense."

9. These experts say that responsive parents prove to babies that they can count on their mother and father this trust is crucial to children's well-being and development.

10. Pediatrician William Sears says that parents should put themselves in the crying child's position and ask what they would want the mother or father to do, he is sure the answer would be to pick up the child.

21-3: Correcting a Run-On by Adding a Comma and a Conjunction

In the following items, correct the run-ons and comma splices by adding a coordinating conjunction (*and, but, or, so, for, nor, yet*).

EXAMPLE

　　　　　　　　　　　　　　　　　　　　　　　　　, but
I know that movies can be unrealistic ᴧI still love to watch them.

1. Don't believe everything you learn about animals from Hollywood movies you might come away misinformed.

2. For example, the 1994 movie *Andre the Seal* is based on a true story about a New England harbor seal, the title character is played by a California sea lion.

3. The real Andre was five feet long and weighed 250 pounds the sea lion actor is twice as big.

4. The decision to cast a solid-brown sea lion as a spotted gray seal may seem ridiculous, the filmmakers had their reasons.

5. Unlike sea lions, harbor seals don't have huge front flippers, they can't scoot around very well.

6. Seals can't do cute tricks on land with human actors, they spend most of their time in the water.

7. In the 1995 movie *Outbreak*, a monkey brings a deadly African virus to America the monkey is actually played by a South American capuchin monkey.

8. That's because capuchins are more readily available than African monkeys, they are easier to train.

9. You might assume that the 1988 movie *Gorillas in the Mist* portrays animals accurately, it was filmed on location in Africa among a band of mountain gorillas.

10. However, wild mother gorillas won't let humans touch their young in one scene a baby gorilla is really a chimpanzee in a gorilla suit.

21-4: Correcting a Run-On by Adding a Dependent Word

In the following items, correct the run-ons and comma splices by adding a dependent word (*after, while, as, because, before, although, even though, if, that, though, unless, when, who, which, where*) to make a dependent clause. Add or delete a comma if necessary.

EXAMPLE

because

Being a working mother is difficult,/work and school schedules often conflict.

1. Kristin Hersh is a working mother, she has a rather unusual job.

2. Hersh is raising her children, she has both a solo career and is the lead singer and guitarist for the band Throwing Muses.

3. Her husband, Billy O'Connell, understands her unconventional career choice he's the band's manager.

4. Hersh has combined rock and roll and motherhood, she had her first child at the age of nineteen.

5. Her oldest son Dylan now lives with his father most of the year, he spends vacations with his mother and stepfather.

6. Hersh goes on tour, sons Ryder, Wyatt, and Bodhi will be traveling with their parents.

7. Hersh thinks the rock world is beginning to change it is still uncommon to see children on the tour bus.

8. More women performers are becoming mothers, more kids are being nursed backstage and rocked to sleep in dressing rooms.

9. Hersh and O'Connell waited to let their older sons watch their mom perform most shows are so loud and smoky.

10. The boys watched a smoke-free acoustic show Hersh was pregnant.

21-5: Run-Ons Review (1)

In the following items, correct the run-ons and comma aplices by adding a period, a conjunction, a semicolon, or a dependent word. Add a comma if necessary.

EXAMPLE

Although s

$\stackrel{}{\cancel{S}}$ome inventions are created to solve one person's particular problem,

they can still be of great benefit to others.

1. Nathan Kane began inventing he was eighteen years old.

2. Kane wanted to create a dust-free environment in their Texas home his father suffered from allergies.

3. Ten years later, he won a $30,000 prize for young inventors, the award was presented by the Massachusetts Institute of Technology.

4. Kane was a graduate student at MIT, he was studying mechanical engineering.

5. He thought of the idea for one of his inventions he was refinishing the floors in his parents' house.

6. It was very hot, he was uncomfortable wearing a regular filter mask.

7. Kane invented a mask that supplies fresh air through a flexible hose, the hose is really a lightweight bellows.

8. Bellows have been used for thousands of years, Kane came up with a better design.

9. He and a friend invented a TV remote control that's hard to lose and easy to pass around, it's built inside a foam rubber football.

10. Kane recently served as an adviser to a group of middle-school students, they designed solar-powered model cars.

21-6: Run-Ons Review (2)

In the following items, correct the run-ons and comma splices by adding a period, a conjunction, a semicolon, or a dependent word. Add a comma if necessary.

EXAMPLE

I don't have a degree in business, *but* I want to start my own company someday anyway.

1. Tom Scott and Tom First began selling juice in 1989 they were twenty-four years old.

2. They had been friends since freshman year in college, they moved to the island of Nantucket soon after graduation.

3. Their business began as a floating juice bar in Nantucket Harbor they sold glasses of homemade peach juice off the deck of their boat.

4. Soon Scott and First began bottling their juice by hand, the following summer it was being professionally packaged in New York and distributed throughout Nantucket, Martha's Vineyard, and Cape Cod.

5. Their juice is called Nantucket Nectars, the name of their company is Nantucket Allserve.

6. Sales and production increased dramatically over the next few years, the company was still struggling to survive.

7. In 1993, an investor bought half the company for $500,000, that money allowed Scott and First to expand their markets and product line.

8. Scott and First have no formal business training, Nantucket Allserve was one of the nation's fastest-growing private companies.

9. Their juice is sold in more than forty states the company is worth $30 million.

10. The company is now owned by the Dr. Pepper Snapple Group, Scott and First still voice the radio ads.

Chapter 22: Subject-Verb Agreement

22-1: Correcting Subject-Verb Agreement Problems with the Verbs *Be, Have,* and *Do*

In the following sentences, circle the subject and underline the correct form of the verb in parentheses.

EXAMPLE

The (weather) in New England (is, are) very unpredictable.

1. Believe it or not, the region (was, were) the victim of an amazing April Fool's joke—an enormous blizzard.

2. According to the TV news, it (was, were) the biggest snowstorm to hit Massachusetts since 1978 and the third biggest ever.

3. This blizzard (has, have) to be the worst that I can remember.

4. I (doesn't, don't) know exactly how much snow fell, but in my neighborhood I think we got about 2 feet.

5. Schools (is, are) closed everywhere today because of the snow on the roads.

6. I (has, have) no idea when our street will be plowed.

7. All my neighbors (is, are) outside shoveling or playing in the snow.

8. My family (has, have) a lot of shoveling to do.

9. Some people (has, have) no electricity or phone service because falling trees knocked down power lines.

10. I (am, is, are) pretty sure school will be canceled tomorrow, too.

22-2: Correcting Subject-Verb Agreement Problems When the Subject and Verb Are Separated by a Prepositional Phrase

In the following sentences, cross out any prepositional phrases between a subject and verb, and then underline the correct form of the verb in parentheses.

EXAMPLE

Although women ~~in this century~~ (<u>face</u>, faces) less discrimination than ever before, they still encounter many obstacles that men do not.

1. Gender discrimination in hiring practices (is, are) often hard to prove.

2. It would be easier to prove if you could compare hiring outcomes when the gender of job applicants (is, are) known and when that gender is unknown.

3. Exactly this type of comparison between hiring outcomes (is, are) now complete for one group of employers—U.S. symphony orchestras.

4. A new study of orchestra hiring practices (finds, find) that women are more likely to get a seat in a major orchestra if they audition anonymously.

5. Orchestras throughout the country (uses, use) "blind" auditions to evaluate musicians and have done so since the early 1970s.

6. For the first and semifinal rounds of auditions, applicants for a position with the orchestra (performs, perform) from behind a thick screen to hide their identity from the judges.

7. Economists Claudia Goldin of Harvard University and Cecilia Rouse of Princeton University analyzed data from the late 1950s to 1996 to determine whether blind auditioning at major orchestras (improves, improve) the chances that a woman will be hired.

8. According to Goldin and Rouse, the percentage of female musicians in the top five American orchestras (is, are) 20 percent higher now than it was in 1970.

9. Their study of orchestras (reports, report) that the use of screens boosts by 25 to 45 percent the odds that a woman will be hired.

10. The authors of the study conclude that the switch to blind auditions (explains, explain) about one-third to one-half of the total increase in the percentage of women hired between 1970 and 1996.

22-3: Correcting Subject-Verb Agreement Problems When the Subject and Verb Are Separated by a Dependent Clause

In the following sentences, cross out any dependent clauses between a subject and verb. Then, correct any problems with subject-verb agreement. If there is no problem, write **OK** next to the sentence.

EXAMPLE

Often, people ~~who blindly follow fashion~~ has *have* no idea of the original significance of the trendy item they are wearing.

1. Traditionally, the red dot that Indian women wear on their foreheads indicate that they are married Hindus.

2. This dot, which is known as a *bindi* or *pottu,* represent the mystical "third eye" in Hinduism.

3. The *bindi,* which was originally a simple red or maroon powdered circle, have evolved into a stick-on dot available in a variety of shapes, sizes, and colors.

4. In the 1990s, some women who wore *bindis* were making more of a fashion statement than a religious one.

5. In fact, the religious symbol that Hindu women have worn for centuries are showing up on the foreheads of hip young Americans, both male and female.

6. The American whose *bindi* first attracted attention among trendy, pierced people were probably Gwen Stefani.

7. Stefani, who is the lead singer of the band No Doubt, worn a stick-on *bindi.*

8. Back then, this California rock star, whom many people have compared to Madonna, like to wear a shiny, teardrop-shaped *bindi.*

9. The style that is a favorite among southern Indian women look a bit strange with Stefani's platinum-blonde hair and skintight wardrobe.

10. The *bindi,* which was once a meaningful religious symbol, was just another cool fad.

22-4: Correcting Subject-Verb Agreement Problems with Compound Subjects

In the following sentences, circle the compound subject and then underline the correct form of the verb in parentheses.

EXAMPLE

Although (a human and a cat) (doesn't, <u>don't</u>) seem to have much in common, there are animals with great similarities to humans.

1. The orangutan, gorilla, chimpanzee, and bonobo (is, are) the four species of great apes.

2. Although obviously the chimp and the gorilla (looks, look) more alike, chimpanzees are in fact genetically more similar to humans than to gorillas.

3. In fact, the chimpanzee and the bonobo (shares, share) about 98 percent of the genetic material, or DNA, found in humans.

4. Chimpanzees and humans (is, are) the only two species that deliberately seek out and kill members of their own species.

5. Murder, rape, torture, gang warfare, and territorial raiding (occurs, occur) frequently among chimpanzees.

6. The chimpanzee and the bonobo (is, are) even more closely related to one another than chimps and humans (is, are), yet the bonobo is one of the most peaceful species of mammal.

7. The male and female bonobo (has, have) equal power because the females form alliances that prevent the males from taking control.

8. If a mother bonobo or her son (is, are) attacked, the mother's female allies will chase off the male aggressor.

9. The status or power of a male bonobo usually (depends, depend) on his mother's rank within the group.

10. Today, many scientists disagree over whether the chimpanzee or the bonobo (is, are) more human in its behavior.

22-5: Correcting Subject-Verb Agreement Problems When the Subject Is an Indefinite Pronoun

In the following sentences, circle the subject and cross out any prepositional phrases or dependent clauses that separate it from the verb in parentheses. Then, underline the correct form of that verb.

EXAMPLE

(Anyone) ~~who speaks another language~~ (<u>understands</u>, understand) how difficult it can be to learn a new one.

1. Everyone in my college writing class (speaks, speak) English better than I do.

2. A few of the students (is, are) native speakers of English, but everybody else is learning English as a second language.

3. Many of the students (is, are) from Spanish-speaking places, particularly the Dominican Republic.

4. Several of the best students in the class (is, are) from Haiti, where they grew up speaking a dialect of French called Creole.

5. One of my closest friends in the class (comes, come) from Korea and moved here just six months ago.

6. Both of us (lives, live) with our parents, and we commute to school on the same bus.

7. No one who is in my class (speaks, speak) English the way you hear it spoken on television and in the movies.

8. Each of us (studies, study) hard, but I think that I work the hardest.

9. Unfortunately, none of my hard work (seems, seem) to have paid off yet.

10. Neither of my parents (speaks, speak) much English, so maybe that's why I'm having such a hard time.

22-6: Correcting Subject-Verb Agreement Problems When the Verb Comes before the Subject

In the following sentences, correct any problems with subject-verb agreement. If there is no problem, write **OK** next to the sentence.

EXAMPLE

Included in the course requirements ~~are~~ *is* a research paper.

1. Here is the first two pages of the essay that you promised to look over for me.

2. There are two more pages that I'm not ready to show you yet.

3. Has you helped other students with their papers before?

4. There is probably lots of mistakes in grammar, punctuation, and spelling.

5. Is this the worst paper you have ever seen?

6. In your opinion, what is my paper's biggest problems?

7. Is papers like this always difficult for freshmen like me?

8. Does other students go to the Writing Center for help?

9. I heard there is computers that we can use in the Center.

10. There is a friend of mine who might also need your help, if that's all right with you.

22-7: Subject-Verb Agreement Review

In each of the following sentences, underline the subject and circle the correct form of the verb in parentheses.

EXAMPLE

<u>Going</u> to work ((is,) are) sometimes like following an obstacle course.

1. Commuting (is, are) a hassle for just about everyone.

2. Many (has, have) to race against time and traffic to make it to work or to school on time.

3. Travel within cities (has become, have become) easier with increased public transportation.

4. However, commuting in the snow or the rain (remain, remains) a problem even for those who take a train, bus, or subway.

5. Businesses around the country (continue, continues) to experiment with telecommuting as an option for their employees.

6. Telecommuters, who set up an office equipped with a computer, fax machine, second telephone line, and e-mail, (works, work) productively without having to leave home.

7. Companies that have spent time and money rethinking "the office" (reports, report) that telecommuters are no less productive than their in-office counterparts.

8. Collaboration and feedback (happen, happens) electronically through employee e-mail accounts and networking technology.

9. Community colleges and universities (is, are) taking their cue from business and offering classes by distance learning.

10. (Has, Have) you heard about some of these alternative ways of commuting?

Chapter 23: Verb Tense

23-1: Using the Correct Verb Form for Regular Verbs in the Present Tense

For each of the sentences below, fill in the blank with the correct present-tense form of the verb in parentheses.

EXAMPLE

I _____*want*_____ (to want) to learn how to live a long, healthy life.

1. Doctors _____ (to explain) that exercise plays an important part in staying healthy.

2. Some days, I _____ (to stop) at the gym to work out.

3. When I am there, I usually _____ (to use) the Stairmaster and the rowing machine.

4. My gym also _____ (to offer) classes in kickboxing, yoga, and aerobics.

5. Many people _____ (to take) these classes because they prefer to exercise in groups.

6. I suppose that they _____ (to feel) it's easier to stay motivated when there is an instructor telling them what to do.

7. My friend Karen _____ (to love) taking karate classes.

8. On nice days in the spring and fall, I _____ (to prefer) to run or ride my bicycle outside for exercise.

9. Lots of people who do not exercise much _____ (to think) that people who do so are just worried about their weight.

10. However, exercising several times a week _____ (to keep) me feeling energetic and strong.

23-2: Using the Correct Verb Form for Regular Verbs in the Past Tense

For each of the sentences below, fill in the blank with the correct past-tense form of the verb in parentheses.

EXAMPLE

Rhodesian Ridgebacks, a playful and sociable breed, ___*hunted*___ (to hunt) lions alongside their masters on the plains of Africa and were once called African Lion Hounds.

1. The dogs that we know today as house pets once _____ (to specialize) in certain tasks that made them invaluable to humans.

2. For example, Saint Bernards _____ (to rescue) avalanche victims in the Alps.

3. Similarly, the Alaskan malamute _____ (to pull) sleds in freezing weather.

4. The Doberman pinscher's strength, speed, and courage _____ (to result) in their use as police dogs.

5. Irish wolfhounds, also strong and fast, _____ (to use) their powerful jaws to hold wolves by the neck and shake them until they died.

6. Even breeds such as the terriers and spaniels _____ (to help) humans.

7. The Scottish terrier _____ (to chase) rats and badgers away from people's homes.

8. Little cocker spaniels _____ (to scare) birds out of bushes and trees so that they could be hunted.

9. The ever-popular Labrador retriever not only _____ (to retrieve) hunted animals on land but could also swim in icy waters.

10. Their tireless assistance and love for their masters _____ (to earn) dogs the well-known title of "man's best friend."

23-3: Using the Correct Verb Form for Regular Verbs in the Present Tense and Past Tense

In the following sentences, fill in the correct form and tense of the verb in parentheses.

EXAMPLE

I _____wish_____ (to wish) that finding a job were easier to do.

1. Recently, I _____ (to apply) for a job as an administrative assistant at an insurance company.

2. I _____ (to hope) to hear something soon because I really need a job.

3. Before I found this job notice, I _____ (to search) everywhere I could think of.

4. I _____ (to check) all the help wanted ads in the newspaper.

5. My sister _____ (to show) me how to look for jobs on the Internet.

6. She still _____ (to help) me find a new Internet site to check every day.

7. I _____ (to want) to have a job before the end of the summer.

8. My tuition _____ (to increase) a lot last semester.

9. I _____ (to need) to make enough money to pay it.

10. My books _____ (to cost) a lot, too.

23-4: Using the Correct Verb Forms for *Be* and *Have* in the Present Tense

In the following sentences, fill in the correct present-tense form of the verb in parentheses.

EXAMPLE

A well-written cover letter _____*is*_____ (to be) an important part of a job application.

1. I _____ (to be) interested in applying for the part-time sales position you advertised in last Sunday's *Gazette*.

2. As you can see from my résumé, I _____ (to have) two years' experience working in retail sales.

3. Last year I worked as a sales associate at Jeans R Us, and I _____ (to be) now the assistant weekend store manager at Clothes to the Bone.

4. As you know, both stores _____ (to have) excellent reputations for customer satisfaction.

5. In addition to my professional experience in sales, I _____ (to be) currently a student at Green Valley Community College.

6. Because I _____ (to be) a marketing major, I feel that my academic work helps qualify me for a sales position at your store.

7. I _____ (to have) a 3.2 grade point average and have been on the Dean's List for the past two semesters.

8. I would particularly like to work at your store because it _____ (to have) such a strong commitment to environmental and social issues.

9. I hope that if the job _____ (to be) still open, you will consider me a serious candidate.

10. I will call you next week to see if you _____ (to be) interested in arranging an interview.

23-5: Using the Correct Forms for Irregular Verbs in the Past Tense (1)

In the following sentences, fill in the blank with the correct past-tense form of the irregular verb in parentheses.

EXAMPLE

Sports heroes _____*had*_____ (to have) a strong influence on me when I was a child.

1. Tiger Woods, the most successful young golfer in the history of the sport, _____ (to grow) up in Cypress, California.

2. He _____ (to begin) learning golf when he was only six months old, watching his father practice swings in the garage.

3. Four months later, Tiger _____ (to take) his own first swing with a sawed-off club.

4. When he _____ (to be) a year and a half old, Tiger would practice hitting at the driving range.

5. While other toddlers played in sandboxes, Tiger _____ (to hit) chip shots out of sand traps.

6. His parents _____ (to bring) him up strictly, yet they never pushed him into stardom.

7. Beginning when Tiger was very young, his father _____ (to teach) him to take responsibility for his own actions and to live by the rules.

8. As a teenager, Tiger tried playing baseball, basketball, football, and track, but he _____ (to quit) these other sports because they interfered with golf.

9. Growing up in a family of mixed racial heritage—Native American, African American, Chinese, Thai, and white—he _____ (to know) about the racism his father had experienced in college and the military.

10. In one of his first ads for Nike, Tiger _____ (to say) that there are still twenty-three golf courses in the United States where he is not allowed to play because of the color of his skin.

23-6: Using the Correct Forms for Irregular Verbs in the Past Tense (2)

For each of the following sentences, fill in the blank with the correct past-tense form of the irregular verb in parentheses.

EXAMPLE

My grandmother _____*was*_____ (to be) a great baker and an even better cook.

1. When I was growing up, I _____ (to eat) differently than I do now.

2. My mother _____ (to make) fried chicken with mashed potatoes and gravy every Saturday.

3. We never _____ (to think) about cholesterol or calories.

4. Then, ten years ago my older brother John _____ (to have) a heart attack.

5. His wife _____ (to bring) him to the hospital immediately, and luckily the doctors were able to save his life.

6. The surgeon _____ (to say) that if John had arrived at the hospital five minutes later than he did, he probably wouldn't be alive today.

7. John _____ (to know) that he had to lose weight and change his diet dramatically.

8. He _____ (to lose) eighty pounds in seven months, bringing him to a healthy weight.

9. He _____ (to tell) me that I should begin to eat a healthier diet and lose weight, too.

10. I _____ (to quit) eating a lot of the foods I was used to, but I have found many new favorites.

23-7: Using the Correct Forms for the Past Participles of Regular Verbs

For each of the following sentences, fill in the blank with the correct past participle form of the verb in parentheses.

EXAMPLE

Having a college degree has ___*benefited*___ (to benefit) me immensely in my job search.

1. These days, many people have _____ (to try) a few different job options before they settle on a profession.

2. Those people who have _____ (to work) part time in high school or college have gotten a taste of working life.

3. I have _____ (to wait) on tables at my neighborhood restaurant, Taco Loco, for the past year.

4. This work has _____ (to help) me to see that I do not like working with difficult customers.

5. In addition to working as a waitress, I also have _____ (to park) cars at a fancy hotel.

6. Part-time jobs have _____ (to prepare) me to join the full-time workforce.

7. They have _____ (to allow) me to see what I am good at and what I most enjoy.

8. I have _____ (to realize) that I might prefer machines to people.

9. As a result, I have _____ (to register) for classes in computer technology.

10. This field has _____ (to expand) enormously in the last decade and should be both lucrative and enjoyable for me.

23-8: Using the Correct Forms for the Past Participles of Irregular Verbs

For each of the following sentences, fill in the blank with the correct past participle form of the irregular verb in parentheses.

EXAMPLE

Many people have _____seen_____ (to see) TV shows about dance competitions.

1. I have _____ (to begin) to see why everyone is raving about these TV shows.

2. *Dancing with the Stars* has _____ (to become) extremely popular over the last several years.

3. People all over the country have _____ (to catch) on to the show that is changing how people view dancing.

4. These shows have _____ (to create) new interest in ball-room dancing.

5. In the past, I have _____ (to find) many musicals to be unrealistic.

6. The producers of these dance shows have _____ (to do) a wonderful job of creating interest in what will happen next.

7. They have _____ (to seek) celebrities who have the potential to really learn to dance.

8. The celebrities have _____ (to show) the ability to learn a new and difficult skill.

9. I have _____ (to fall) into a routine of watching these shows with friends.

10. People like us have _____ (to make) *Dancing with the Stars* as popular as many of the dramas on television.

23-9: Using the Present Perfect Tense (1)

In the following sentences, underline the correct tense of the verb in parentheses. Choose between the past tense and present perfect tense.

EXAMPLE

Over the course of my life, I (changed, <u>have changed</u>) direction more than once.

1. When I graduated from high school back in 1994, I (was, have been) not interested in going to college.

2. Instead, I got married and (became, have become) a mother right away.

3. For the past eighteen years, I (stayed, have stayed) home to raise my three children.

4. When my youngest child entered high school last September, I (began, have begun) thinking about what it would be like to have my own career.

5. Until recently, my family (got, has gotten) by on my husband's paycheck.

6. Then Tom (lost, has lost) his job after sixteen years with the same company.

7. Since the layoff, he (applied, has applied) for more than one hundred jobs but can find only part-time work that doesn't pay very well.

8. After much discussion, we finally (decided, have decided) that I should go back to school to become a paralegal.

9. For the past semester I (attended, have attended) Mt. Ida College.

10. Though I enjoy my classes, at first it (felt, have felt) strange to be a student again.

23-10: Using the Present Perfect Tense (2)

For each of the following sentences, fill in the blank with the correct present perfect form of the verb in parentheses.

EXAMPLE

Current events _have reinforced_ (to reinforce) my fear of flying.

1. A number of recent crashes _____ (to raise) questions about the risks of letting new pilots fly at night.

2. The National Transportation Safety Board _____ (to investigate) the circumstances surrounding these fatal crashes.

3. The Board _____ (to state) that approximately eighty people die each year in crashes of privately flown planes.

4. Evidence _____ (to show) that disorientation is a major risk for inexperienced pilots.

5. Nevertheless, the Federal Aviation Administration _____ (to announce) that the current rules for new pilots are adequate.

6. Some experts _____ (to argue) that these types of crashes have decreased in number over the last twenty years.

7. Other countries, such as Great Britain, _____ (to create) laws that require new pilots to have special instruments for flying at night.

8. In many cases, these instruments _____ (to help) disoriented pilots distinguish the earth from the sky.

9. As a result, the instruments _____ (to prevent) pilots from crashing into the earth.

10. Many Americans _____ (to write) to their representatives and senators to try to get similar legislation passed in the United States.

23-11: Using the Past Perfect Tense (1)

In the following sentences, underline the correct tense of the verb in parentheses. Choose between the past tense and the past perfect tense.

EXAMPLE

Just when I thought I had it all figured out, life (<u>threw</u>, had thrown) me another curve ball.

1. Before I (became, had become) a student at Hudson Valley Community College this fall, I had been a stay-at-home mother for nine years.

2. I (thought, had thought) about going back to school ever since my sister got her degree in 2006.

3. Yet, until my husband and I split up two years ago, I (saw, had seen) no way to make such a dramatic change in my life.

4. I (was, had been) divorced for six months before I even began to apply to colleges.

5. At first I (tried, had tried) to get a job without going back to school, but that plan gradually fell apart.

6. The only jobs I (found, had found) didn't even pay enough to cover my childcare expenses.

7. I (worked, had worked) as a secretary before I quit to have kids.

8. When I (stopped, had stopped) working in 1991, I had never even used a computer.

9. If I (knew, had known) that I would one day be a single mother, I would never have left the workforce.

10. On the other hand, I guess that if I (kept, had kept) working, I would never have gone to college.

23-12: Using the Past Perfect Tense (2)

For each of the following sentences, fill in the blank with the correct past perfect form of the verb in parentheses.

EXAMPLE

When I asked my grandfather about his career, I ___*had guessed*___ (to guess) correctly that he would have a long and interesting story to tell.

1. When my grandfather retired at the age of seventy, he _____ (to hold) many different jobs.

2. By the time he was fifteen years old, he _____ (to drop out) of school and was working full time at a pizzeria.

3. Before he was a chef at the pizzeria, though, he _____ (to be) a tailor at the shop across the street.

4. When he married my grandmother at the age of eighteen, he _____ (to work) at four different restaurants and bakeries.

5. He left each job after a short time because he _____ (to figure out) that there would be a better wage at another one.

6. Before my uncle was born, my grandfather _____ (to realize) that he was going to have to try something else yet again in order to support his rapidly growing family.

7. His own father _____ (to manage) grocery stores for a living, and he decided to give that kind of job a try.

8. The grocery store business was very good to him, and by the time he moved to Florida forty years later he _____ (to receive) more than twenty-five promotions and raises.

9. My grandfather always says that what he wishes he _____ (to learn) earlier is that there is often more to gain sticking with one job than bouncing around.

10. I'm not sure that this is always true, though, and I might not have found the great job I have now if I _____ (not to try) a couple of other ones first.

23-13: Identifying Active and Passive Voice

In each of the following sentences, underline the subject once and the verb twice, and indicate whether the sentence is active or passive by writing **A** or **P** in the space provided.

EXAMPLE

_____P_____ I <u>was asked</u> by my former teacher to talk to her class about how I began my career as a computer technician.

1. _____ I completed a certificate program in computer science one year ago.

2. _____ A lot was taught by my teacher about different computer platforms, software, and networks.

3. _____ It was suggested to me by my teacher that I start looking for a job before I finished the program.

4. _____ Letters were sent out to the technical support departments of several companies asking about job openings.

5. _____ In the letters, I mentioned that I would soon finish the certificate program and that I had also done extra research about the computer industry on my own.

6. _____ Form letters were sent by a few companies that had no job openings.

7. _____ Several companies called me to come in for interviews.

8. _____ A part-time job was offered by one company until I finished school and could start full-time.

9. _____ Of course, I accepted the company's offer.

10. _____ Skilled and motivated technical support workers are needed by practically every company these days.

23-14: Using Active Voice

Revise each of the following sentences to change passive voice to active voice.

EXAMPLE

It has been decided by the students that the increase in parking rates is unfair.

The students have decided that the increase in parking rates is unfair.

1. A poll was taken by several student organizations that are working together to oppose the increase in parking rates.

2. It was voted by 90 percent of the students who drive to school that the increase is too high.

3. "The rates were already high, and now they have more than doubled," was remarked by one student.

4. That the state has given the college less money this year is recognized by the students.

5. Students who drive to school should not be forced by the college to make up the entire amount of money cut by the state.

6. In most cases, driving to school is resorted to only by students who don't live near public transportation.

7. Paying the increased rate will be found impossible by some of these students.

8. Not enough time is had by students who come to class after work to drive to a subway station and then take the subway to school.

9. Some people may be discouraged from applying to the college at all by the expensive parking rates.

10. Funds should be raised by the college in a way that is fair to all students.

23-15: Using the Passive Voice

Rewrite each of the following sentences using the passive voice.

EXAMPLE

The library is enforcing a new policy.

A new policy is being enforced by the library.

1. We should not bring drinks or food into the library.

2. I brought a drink into the library the other day.

3. My friend spilled the drink on a book.

4. Someone found the ruined book on Tuesday.

5. This person reported my friend and me to the librarians.

6. The authorities revoked our library cards the following day.

7. They denied us the chance to plead our case.

8. A professor who heard about our case told the dean how unfair it was.

9. No one actually saw us spill the drink on the book.

10. The law states that rights and privileges cannot be revoked based on circumstantial evidence.

23-16: Correcting Problems with Consistency of Verb Tense

In the following sentences, select the proper form of the verb to maintain consistency of tense throughout the set of sentences. Remember that sometimes shifts in tense are logical.

EXAMPLE

Beach volleyball players seldom (<u>achieve</u>, achieved) fame in the United States, but today there (<u>is</u>, was) an exception.

1. Misty May-Treanor (is, was) definitely famous to many for her three Olympic victories.

2. In 2004, she (wins, won) her first gold medal.

3. The Olympic tournament (is, was) grueling for most athletes, but May-Treanor (is, was) not a typical athlete.

4. In 2012, at the age of 35, she (became, becomes) the first three-time medal winner in the history of her sport.

5. Commentators (consider, considered) her and her partner, Kerri Walsh Jennings, the greatest beach volleyball team ever.

6. After winning her second gold medal in 2008, she (endures, endured) a serious Achilles tendon injury on *Dancing with the Stars*.

7. She (returns, returned) to beach volleyball competition in 2009.

8. Her success (is, was) not only evident in her athletic achievements.

9. To help people less fortunate than herself, she (has, had) served as a sports ambassador for the Special Olympics.

10. In 2004, she (marries, married) baseball player Matt Treanor, and the two of them now (lived, live) in Florida and California.

23-17: Using Consistent Verb Tense

For each of the following sentences, fill in the blank with the form of the verb in parentheses that is consistent with the other verbs in the sentence.

EXAMPLE

As the Internet has become more familiar over the past fifteen

years, the number of Internet users _has increased_ (to increase)

dramatically.

1. Many people shop over the Internet and _____ (to read) about topics that interest them.

2. One woman who had been set up on a blind date ran an Internet search on her beau and _____ (to find) that he had been described in an online article as one of the ten worst dates of all time.

3. People are concerned about privacy on the Internet and _____ (to ask) questions about Internet security.

4. The Internet has made knowledge more available but also _____ (to raise) new questions about the boundaries between private and public information.

5. Many articles have argued that we are losing our privacy and _____ (to give) examples of what average people do on the Internet.

6. People order books or _____ (to listen) to music online and reveal potentially important information about themselves to corporations.

7. Teens talk about personal things on Facebook and sometimes _____ (to post) revealing pictures.

8. Authorities and parents worry that such teens _____ (to be) at risk of being stalked by dangerous people.

9. Some people _____ (to erase) their Internet transactions and other activities with special software that costs a great deal of money.

10. But most of us do not buy this software and _____ (to be) at risk of having our personal preferences and interests becoming public information.

23-18: Verb Problems Review

In the following sentences, fill in the correct form and tense of the verb in parentheses.

EXAMPLE

Many great works of art _____*are*_____ (to be) in danger of being destroyed by time.

1. Leonardo da Vinci _____ (to be) probably the world's most famous artist.

2. His reputation as an inventor, scientist, and engineer _____ (to grow) tremendously over the years.

3. You may _____ (to see) a copy of his painting the *Mona Lisa*.

4. The original painting at the Louvre Museum in Paris _____ (to lie) behind a thick sheet of bulletproof glass.

5. Da Vinci _____ (to paint) another of his famous works, the *Last Supper*, on the wall of a church in Milan, Italy, in 1497.

6. Unfortunately, this great painting _____ (to decay) badly over time.

7. In fact, the *Last Supper* _____ (to begin) to fall apart almost immediately after Leonardo _____ (to finish) it.

8. He _____ (to use) an experimental technique that _____ (to give) him more time to work but _____ (to make) the painting crack and peel.

9. Since 1726, there _____ (to be) many disastrous attempts to restore the *Last Supper*.

10. Luckily, a conservation effort that _____ (to begin) in 1977 _____ (to reverse) some of the damage.

Chapter 24: Pronouns

24-1: Identifying Pronouns

Underline the pronoun or pronouns in each of the following sentences.

EXAMPLE

"Take This Job and Shove <u>It</u>" was once a popular country song by Johnny Paycheck.

1. Today, nearly 10 percent of all Americans are unemployed.

2. Workers must work harder now than they did in the past because of a tougher labor market.

3. Employees know that they need skills more than ever before.

4. One grocery store employee recently said she needed a raise but would hesitate to quit if she did not receive one.

5. Workers like her know that they cannot easily find jobs elsewhere.

6. In recent years, American workers had averaged three years of working at their place of business.

7. Industries such as food services currently saw their worst employee turnover rates ever.

8. The food services industries often provide dead-end, boring, or dangerous jobs that leave their workers dissatisfied.

9. Industry leaders have seen a change with the economic downturn, and they are concerned.

10. Employers and job seekers hope that they will see a change soon.

24-2: Making Pronouns Agree with Indefinite Pronouns and Collective Nouns

In the following sentences, underline the correct pronoun or pronouns from the choices in parentheses.

EXAMPLE

If a student group is really dedicated to a particular cause, (<u>it</u>, they) can help bring about change.

1. My college just announced that (it, they) will be raising tuition next year.

2. This is terrible news for anyone who has to pay (his or her, their) own way.

3. Someone wrote a letter to the editor of the school paper saying that (she, they) would have to drop out of college if tuition went up.

4. Several other letter-writers said that (he or she, they) had no idea how to come up with the extra money.

5. "Society needs to turn (its, their) attention to the fact that ordinary people can no longer afford a college education," wrote one angry student.

6. A group calling (itself, themselves) Students Against Soaring Tuition (SAST) held a protest rally outside the president's office, and the crowd chanted slogans for three hours.

7. Both my parents work hard at (his or her job, their jobs), but neither of them can afford to pay so much money for my education.

8. My family does all (it, they) can to pay the rent and grocery bill each month.

9. The financial aid office said that (it, they) won't be able to increase my loan for next year.

10. Luckily, however, the jewelry company where I worked part-time last summer promised that (it, they) would give me more hours this summer.

24-3: Making Pronouns Agree with Indefinite Pronouns

Fill in the blank with the correct pronoun in each of the following sentences.

EXAMPLE

Someone who puts ___*his or her*___ life at risk for others is a hero.

1. Everyone remembers where _____ was on September 11, 2001.

2. At my school, several of the teachers turned on the television sets in _____ classrooms.

3. Everybody put _____ things away in a locker and crowded into a room with a television.

4. No one could believe _____ eyes at what was happening.

5. Each student sat with _____ mouth open.

6. Many could not leave _____ seats even after class ended.

7. Our teacher had been talking about our test results, and everyone had crossed _____ fingers hoping for good news.

8. Few could forget how confused _____ were by the first announcements about the attacks.

9. The day after, many of us said _____ could not sleep that night.

10. The newspapers and television news both made the attacks _____ lead story for months.

24-4: Making Pronouns Agree with Collective Nouns

For each of the following sentences, fill in the blank with the correct pronoun.

EXAMPLE

A company on the Internet will let people search _____*its*_____ records for information about their ancestors.

1. My mother's family has had _____ history recorded in several different books because her descendants were slaves of one of the wealthiest plantations in Mississippi.

2. Our local historical society asked if _____ could have permission to research and write about our family.

3. The college in the town where my great-grandfather was born holds much information about my family in _____ library.

4. The government of Mississippi kept records of all of _____ citizens and their property.

5. Because slaves were considered property, the group of authors and researchers from the historical society was able to find the information _____ needed in those records.

6. A committee that helps to retrieve historical information about slaves offered _____ assistance to the authors in gathering data.

7. When the books were published, the publishing company asked if _____ could host a meeting with the authors to lecture about their findings.

8. When we got to the meeting, the audience was enormous and had lined _____ up outside the meeting hall waiting to get in.

9. A team of journalists waited _____ turn to take pictures of our family.

10. The crowd got to hear what _____ had come for—my mother's moving speech about her family and the authors' recounting of what they found about her descendants.

24-5: Avoiding Ambiguous, Vague, or Repetitious Pronoun References

Edit each sentence to eliminate any ambiguous, vague, or repetitious pronoun references. Some sentences may be revised in more than one way.

EXAMPLE

Insurance policies can be difficult to understand, especially when ~~they~~ *insurance companies* don't offer good customer service.

1. Yesterday, I got a letter from my doctor informing me that they were no longer accepting my insurance plan.

2. Dr. Reuter and her partner, Dr. Spingarn, have decided not to go along with the insurance company's new way of paying doctors.

3. According to the letter, my insurance company is now forcing doctors to accept capitation, a payment method that it describes as "unethical."

4. With this payment method, every month the doctor gets a fixed fee for each patient, no matter how much treatment he or she provides.

5. In other words, doctors are paid the same amount whether they need six office visits a month or none.

6. With the traditional fee-for-service method of reimbursing doctors, insurance companies pay every time they treat a patient.

7. My doctor and her partner believe that capitation is bad because they reward doctors for providing less medical care and penalize them for providing more.

8. They think it creates a conflict of interest between doctors and patients because they have a financial incentive to withhold treatment.

9. Dr. Reuter and Dr. Spingarn decided that they could not accept the capitation plan even if it meant losing patients who could not switch to a different insurance company.

10. When I called my insurance company to complain about capitation, they told me that they were simply trying to keep my premiums down by controlling medical costs.

24-6: Using the Right Type of Pronoun with Compound Subjects and Objects

Edit the following sentences to ensure that the proper type of pronoun is used. If a sentence is already correct, write **OK** next to it.

EXAMPLE

Sometimes day-to-day problems can put stress on a marriage, but

my husband and ~~me~~ ^I always talk over a problem until it is solved.

1. Last March, my friend Elena and me both had babies, five days apart.

2. Everyone in the neighborhood gave Elena and I a double baby shower, with matching outfits for our two kids.

3. During the summer Elena and I used to spend a lot of time together, pushing Max and Lucy in their strollers and sitting in the park.

4. Unfortunately, now that I'm in school and Elena is back at her job, me and her don't see each other as much as we used to.

5. Sometimes, me and Max run into her and Lucy at the playground or the library.

6. When we saw Lucy and her the other day, Elena was complaining that her and her husband, Danny, never spend any time together anymore.

7. They're always so tired and stressed out from working and taking care of Lucy that when her and Danny do see each other, they just end up arguing.

8. Elena thinks it would be a good idea for her and Danny to go away for a long weekend without the baby.

9. The other day she said, "If things don't get better between he and I, Danny and me are going to end up getting a divorce."

10. I told her that me and David had struggled with the same issue and that I thought they would work things out if they could just spend more time together.

24-7: Using the Right Type of Pronoun in Comparisons

Edit the following sentences to ensure that the proper type of pronoun is used. If a sentence is already correct, write **OK** next to it. Some sentences may have more than one error.

EXAMPLE

I try not to be too competitive with my brother because I already

know that I can do everything better than ~~him~~.
          he
                                                        ^

1. My older sister, Nadine, always seems to get her schoolwork done faster than me.

2. Nadine does better on tests, but I write better papers than her.

3. As a result, she usually gets about the same grades as me.

4. However, I don't think she tries as hard as I or cares as much about school.

5. The whole time we were growing up, teachers always seemed to like her better than I.

6. It drove me crazy that they didn't treat me the same as her.

7. Nadine is eighteen months older than me, but people always ask us if we're twins.

8. Now that we're both in college, I keep wondering if I'm doing as well as she.

9. I guess deep down inside I'm worried that people will respect her more than me or think she's smarter than me.

10. I don't understand why I'm so competitive with Nadine, since I don't know any sisters who are closer friends than us.

24-8: Choosing between *Who* and *Whom*

In the following sentences, underline the correct pronoun, choosing between *who* and *whom* or *whoever* and *whomever*.

EXAMPLE

When a company is interviewing candidates for a job, it looks for the person (<u>who</u>, whom) will best fulfill the job requirements.

1. I had a job interview last week with a woman (who, whom) is the editor of a nutrition newsletter called *You Are What You Eat.*

2. I also met with her assistant, (who, whom) I had spoken to on the phone when I set up the interview.

3. The editor, (who, whom) talked with me for about 20 minutes, described the newsletter and asked me about my interest in working there.

4. She explained that the newsletter had been started four years ago by her boss, (who, whom) used to be a writer for a health and fitness magazine.

5. Her boss, (who, whom) I did not get a chance to meet, is also planning to start a nutrition Web site.

6. The editor said that she is looking for someone (who, whom) has excellent computer skills as well as some experience with desktop publishing software.

7. She said that (whoever, whomever) she decides to hire will help lay out the newsletter and may have some involvement with designing the new Web site.

8. During the interview, I said that I had become interested in nutrition because of my mother, (who, whom) is a dietitian for a hospital.

9. The editor said that she was going to be interviewing several other people, some of (who, whom) have more experience than I do.

10. She asked me to give her the names and phone numbers of two people (who, whom) she could call as references.

24-9: Making Pronouns Consistent in Person

Edit each sentence to ensure that the pronouns are consistent in person.

EXAMPLE

People who set goals for themselves find that ~~you~~ *they* achieve what ~~you~~ *they* set out to do.

1. Many students and professionals do not realize that writing can provide you with a means of achieving goals.

2. They need to understand that writing down your goals is better than just thinking about them.

3. When someone writes down a goal, one part of his or her brain starts collecting pertinent information and sends it to the conscious part of your mind.

4. Thus, the person starts to recognize opportunities you never would have noticed otherwise.

5. When you put your goals on paper, people need to include both short- and long-term goals.

6. People who try this technique should not worry about your spelling or edit your ideas.

7. If students have trouble writing goals, you might want to write down on another sheet what is keeping you from reaching your goals.

8. By being specific rather than vague, people can more easily decide how to meet your goals.

9. To help you focus on the outcome, a person may want to include smaller goals that are steps to the final goal.

10. People who follow this technique have learned that the fears that could keep them from succeeding become more manageable if you write those fears down.

Chapter 25: Adjectives and Adverbs

25-1: Choosing between Adjectives and Adverbs

In the following sentences, underline the correct adjective or adverb in parentheses, and then circle the word it describes, or modifies, in the sentence.

EXAMPLE

Many ancient societies had strong (oral, orally) traditions, meaning that stories were passed on by word of mouth.

1. Every culture tells folktales about a (mischievous, mischievously) character known as the trickster.

2. He is a (greedy, greedily) troublemaker who is always doing something he was told not to do or poking his nose where it doesn't belong.

3. The trickster is (usual, usually) a small animal who has to rely on his wits to survive.

4. His (foolish, foolishly) pranks often backfire, and we learn through his example how we should *not* behave.

5. However, though we reject the trickster's dishonesty, we (secret, secretly) admire his cleverness.

6. We enjoy watching him outsmart his (powerful, powerfully) opponents.

7. In some folktales, the trickster is a hero because his thefts and deceptions turn out to help his people in (unexpected, unexpectedly) ways.

8. The world's most (popular, popularly) tricksters are Reynard the Fox in European folktales, Anansi the spider in West African tales, Brer Rabbit in African American tales, and Coyote in Native American tales.

9. In a story told by the Zuni people of the American Southwest, Coyote persuades his (sensible, sensibly) friend Eagle to help him steal the sun and the moon so that they will have light to hunt by.

10. (Uncontrollable, Uncontrollably) curious, Coyote opens a box containing the sun and the moon and allows them to escape, thus bringing winter into the world.

25-2: Using Comparative and Superlative Forms

In the following sentences, write the correct form of the adjective or adverb in parentheses.

EXAMPLE

Folktales often offer explanations for the _most intriguing_ (intriguing) aspects of the natural world, such as why the sky is blue.

1. Coyote is the _____ (famous) trickster character in Native American folklore, appearing in stories told throughout California, the Southwest, and the Central Plains.

2. He is _____ (famous) than Mink, Raven, or Bluejay, who are the trickster characters among the tribes of the Pacific Northwest.

3. Coyote is the _____ (important) animal of the mythical pre-human animal age, when animals were believed to be able to talk.

4. In many tales he is simply a comical bad guy who thinks he can out-smart all the _____ (strong) animals because he is so much _____ (clever) than the other animals.

5. Even though he is a troublemaker, Coyote sometimes makes life _____ (easy) for people by getting them things they need, such as fire and light.

6. In the Zuni folktale "Coyote Steals the Sun and Moon," Coyote does help people, but he also makes things _____ (hard) for them by introducing winter into the world.

7. Coyote and his friend Eagle encounter the Kachinas, friendly spirits who get their light by opening up two boxes; the _____ (small) one contains the moon, and the _____ (big) one contains the sun.

8. Coyote convinces Eagle that they should steal the sun and the moon, and after the Kachinas fall asleep, Coyote and Eagle add the moon to the _____ (large) box and fly away with it.

9. When Coyote peeks inside the box, the moon immediately escapes into the sky, and the sun flies up even _____ (high).

10. Coyote makes life _____ (difficult) for people because it's his fault that cold and winter come into the world, but he is also responsible for two good things: the coming of light and the natural cycle of the seasons.

25-3: Using *Good, Well, Bad,* and *Badly*

In the following sentences, underline the correct word in parentheses, choosing between *good* and *well* or between the comparative or superlative forms of *good* and *bad*.

EXAMPLE

Some people think that stealing is not wrong if it is done for a (<u>good</u>, well) reason.

1. Coyote, a famous trickster character in Native American folklore, is always up to no (good, well).

2. The Zuni folktale "Coyote Steals the Sun and Moon" tells how Coyote makes life (worse, worst) for people by introducing winter into the world.

3. Because Coyote hunts (bad, badly), he decides to team up with Eagle, who is an excellent hunter.

4. Coyote tells Eagle that it would be (better, best) if the world were not dark because then it would be easier to hunt.

5. When Coyote and Eagle encounter some friendly spirits, the Kachinas, the pair notice that the Kachinas get their light from two boxes—one containing the sun and one containing the moon—and Coyote convinces Eagle that the (better, best) thing to do is to steal the sun and the moon.

6. Eagle then decides that a (good, well) plan is to put the sun and the moon into one box.

7. After Eagle moves the moon into the box with the sun and flies away with it, he refuses to let Coyote carry the box because he knows that things always turn out (bad, badly) when Coyote gets his way.

8. Because Coyote keeps begging to carry the box, Eagle finally gives in, hoping things will turn out (better, best) than he thinks they will.

9. Eagle then fears that the (worse, worst) will happen when Coyote peeks inside the box and the moon and the sun escape into the sky.

10. Although Coyote causes winter to come into the world, the effects of his actions aren't all (bad, badly) because he also brings light to people.

Chapter 26: Misplaced and Dangling Modifiers

26-1: Correcting Misplaced Modifiers

Edit the following sentences to correct any misplaced modifiers.

EXAMPLE

Doing something yourself can ~~both~~ be ^*both* rewarding and educational.

1. We have been building for the past four months an addition onto our house.

2. The addition will be a sunroom that will be entirely lit with almost natural light.

3. Surrounded by windows, I have wanted a room like this one for a long time.

4. We are building the addition using materials recycled from the garage we are tearing down fairly inexpensively.

5. The cedar planks will look charmingly rustic in our new room that once served as the garage siding.

6. We have taken skylights that were once over the bedroom closet and also moved them to the sunroom's roof.

7. We found an old glass door that we can use in our attic for the doorway between the sunroom and the backyard in our attic.

8. Without hesitation, to do the floor ourselves seemed like an impossible job, so we hired a contractor.

9. When we are done with nearly sheet rocking the walls, he can come in and begin laying out the frame for the floor.

10. Soon-to-be-finished, I can't wait until we can begin eating dinner in our new room.

26-2: Correcting Dangling Modifiers

Edit the following sentences to correct any dangling modifiers.

EXAMPLE

passengers on the

Expecting a relaxing day on the water, the ‸boat set sail without worries.

1. Armed and well trained, a yacht where four people were being held hostage yesterday was raided by five elite Coast Guard divers.

2. A woman and her three children, no one was harmed.

3. Scared of the hijacker, the yacht began to sail off its original course.

4. Wanting to go to Greece, the yacht began heading east.

5. Bravely, the hijacker's plans were foiled by a secret message sent to the Coast Guard.

6. Picking up the signal, the action was swift and effective.

7. Distracted by three Coast Guard boats surrounding the front of the yacht, the divers climbed aboard the back of the yacht.

8. Motioning to the hostages to keep quiet, the boats outside kept the hijacker distracted as the ambush started.

9. Unwilling to give in, the firing began.

10. Trained to fire back when necessary, the hijacker was shot.

26-3: Avoiding Misplaced and Dangling Modifiers (1)

Edit the following sentences to eliminate problems with misplaced and dangling modifiers. It may be necessary to add or change words.

EXAMPLE

I find

Not having a car,ₐpublic transportation is very convenient.

1. Getting to work from my house by subway only takes about 20 minutes.

2. While riding the subway, the time passes quickly if you have something to read.

3. I used to take the bus to work instead of the subway, which is slower.

4. The bus nearly takes twice as long as the subway because of all the traffic.

5. Also, the bus almost stops at every corner.

6. Having taken the bus for years, it had never occurred to me to try the subway.

7. Though rather noisy, I prefer the subway because I can read without getting a headache.

8. Riding the subway for a year, I haven't even gotten a headache once.

9. Reading on the bus, my head would start throbbing after 5 minutes.

10. Unable to read, I only could stare out the window.

26-4: Avoiding Misplaced and Dangling Modifiers (2)

Edit the following sentences to eliminate problems with misplaced and dangling modifiers. It may be necessary to add or change words. Some sentences may have more than one error.

EXAMPLE

While gardening in my yard,
ʌI found a kitten that had been abandoned by its motherʌ ~~gardening in my yard.~~

1. Painting our living room, our black cat pushed open the door and rubbed up against the wet molding.

2. Looking like a skunk, we found Lucy hiding under the bed.

3. We had used oil-based paint on the molding, which was now on her fur.

4. We decided to clean her fur with paint thinner after considering our other options.

5. Now covered with paint thinner, we needed to wash and rinse Lucy with soap and water.

6. We realized that we had made a terrible mistake in the basement an hour later cleaning our brushes.

7. Usually so gentle and affectionate, we found Lucy hissing and arching her back at us.

8. Rushing Lucy to the emergency animal hospital, the vet told us that you should never use paint thinner on an animal.

9. We learned that we should have just used soap and water or a lanolin hand cleaner during our conversation with the vet.

10. After being sedated and thoroughly bathed, we took Lucy home, grateful that she was okay.

Chapter 27: Coordination and Subordination

27-1: Coordinating Sentences with Coordinating Conjunctions

Fill in the blank in each sentence with the correct coordinating conjunction (*for, and, nor, but, or, yet, so*).

EXAMPLE

America's landscape is very varied, _____*and*_____ one of the best ways to see it all is to drive across the country.

1. Americans have built dams and rerouted rivers, _____ they have made even the driest parts of the West inhabitable.

2. The Southwest is naturally arid and rocky, _____ we have tried to make it lush and green like the East.

3. The Southwest has a very hot and dry climate, _____ water used for irrigation purposes evaporates and is lost almost as quickly as it is sprayed out of hoses.

4. This means that water is being taken out of streams and rivers without being put back in, _____ the result of such irrigation can be disastrous to natural bodies of water.

5. Damming waterways has effects in the Northwest as well, _____ rivers as far north as Washington State are also artificially rerouted.

6. When rivers are dammed, the salmon that live in them cannot survive, _____ can the bears that depend on the salmon for food.

7. Indian tribes with national rights to the salmon also lose out, _____ the fish that they have depended on for hundreds of years are now becoming extinct.

8. Sport fishermen, environmental groups, and many Indian tribes have asked the government to reconsider its policies about damming waterways, _____ the groups in favor of reallocating rivers and streams have often proved to be more powerful.

9. Many environmentalists have pointed out that we must take better care of our natural waterways, _____ we will lose them and the wildlife dependent on them forever.

10. The late author Wallace Stegner wrote many essays about this subject, _____ in one of them he said, "You have to get over the color green; you have to quit associating beauty with gardens and lawns; you have to get used to an inhuman scale."

27-2: Coordinating Sentences with Semicolons

Combine each of the following pairs of sentences into a single sentence by using a semicolon.

EXAMPLE

Women athletes are demanding the same respect as their male counter-
                         t
parts/They are making their mark in soccer, basketball, and other
      ;

traditionally male sports.

1. Sports that have historically been considered off-limits to women are changing. Women are beginning to participate in professional athletics in areas where they have never competed before.

2. One example is weightlifting. At seventeen, Cheryl Haworth became the most well-known female weightlifter.

3. Haworth is 5 feet 9 inches tall and weighs 300 pounds. She has the ideal build for a weightlifter.

4. She can lift over 300 pounds. This power made her the medal favorite at the 2000 Olympics.

5. She lifts as much as 25 tons in the course of her daily workout. Every day she lifts the equivalent of five elephants or one F-15 fighter jet.

6. Haworth is also something of a practical jokester. She has been known to lift her friend's car and move it to a different location.

7. Haworth's thighs measure 32 inches in circumference. She can bench press 500 pounds.

8. She began lifting weights when she was twelve years old and already weighed 240 pounds. She could lift over 110 pounds.

9. She also has the speed and flexibility needed by a great weightlifter. She can run a 40-yard dash in 5 seconds.

10. Haworth called for significant changes in women's sports. The inclusion of female weightlifting for the first time in the 2000 Olympics was proof of these changes.

27-3: Coordinating Sentences with Semicolons and Conjunctive Adverbs

Combine each of the following pairs of sentences into a single sentence by using a semicolon and a conjunctive adverb (a connecting word or phrase such as *also, as a result, besides, furthermore, however, in addition, in fact, instead, moreover, still, then, therefore*).

EXAMPLE

however, i

A college degree can sometimes seem like an unattainable goal/It is something worth striving for.
;^

1. My friend Simone became pregnant when she was a junior in college. She could not go back to finish her senior year.

2. She could not afford child care. She had to stay home after Danny, her son, was born.

3. Danny is five now and is beginning kindergarten next month. Simone will have 5 hours free every day.

4. Simone has signed up for two morning classes in nursing at her community college. She has applied for a part-time job at a nursing home.

5. It won't be easy fitting work and classes into her busy parenting schedule. Simone feels that Danny will be better off when they are financially secure.

6. There are things she would like to buy for Danny that she cannot afford. Simone wants to show Danny that she can beat the odds.

7. Simone would like to eventually be a nurse. Through caring for Danny, she's already had some practice as one.

8. The three-year course to become a nurse is too much for Simone. She could take fewer classes and become a nurse practitioner.

9. Either way, she would be working with patients. She would be making good use of her naturally caring personality.

10. Simone says she feels more dedicated now than she did five years ago, and so she is glad her schooling was put on hold. She has a wonderful son in her life.

27-4: Using Coordination to Join Two Sentences

Combine each of the following pairs of sentences into a single sentence by using one of the methods of coordination discussed in the chapter: using a comma and a coordinating conjunction, using a semicolon, or using a semicolon and a connecting word or phrase (conjunctive adverb).

EXAMPLE

but i

Owning a car can be convenient and fun, It can also be a big hassle.

1. My car started making a funny noise. I took it to the repair shop down the street.

2. The mechanic told me the car needed a new water pump. He thought it would cost about $300, including labor.

3. My car isn't worth a lot of money. It's probably not worth much more than $300.

4. It's a 1995 Nissan Sentra hatchback with about 130,000 miles. Up until last week it had been driving just fine.

5. Over the years I've had good luck with this car. I've grown quite attached to it.

6. My brother thinks I should get the car repaired. My sister thinks I'd be foolishly throwing good money after bad.

7. My sister is probably right. I'm unhappy about abandoning my car.

8. I could buy my neighbor's 2001 Toyota Corolla. I could go to the used-car dealer my parents recommended.

9. I'm just not sure it makes sense for me to take out a car loan right now. I don't have any money for a down payment.

10. Maybe I should get the car repaired. I could buy a new car after I've saved some money over the summer.

27-5: Using Subordination to Join Two Sentences (1)

Fill in the blank in each sentence with a logical subordinating conjunction.

EXAMPLE

___*Because*___ my sister is a good cook, she has always prepared most of the food for family holidays.

1. _____ she didn't cook when we were very young, she started making cookies, cakes, and some entrees when we were teens.

2. She made us snacks _____ we got home from school.

3. _____ she was working as a cook for a summer job, the chef noticed that she had an excellent sense of how long to cook meats and vegetables on the grill.

4. _____ she finished her shift one night, he offered to give her more training, saying, "You have the potential to be a great cook."

5. _____ he said another word, my sister accepted.

6. _____ she left that job, she has cooked at many more restaurants and recently finished cooking school.

7. At cooking school, she got a scholarship _____ she was such a talented student.

8. _____ she likes to have a break from cooking, she is happy to prepare feasts for family holidays.

9. My spoiled family won't consider an event special _____ my sister prepares her famous chocolate mousse cake.

10. My sister now works at Chez Henri, _____ she uses her fabulous cooking skills.

27-6: Using Subordination to Join Two Sentences (2)

Combine each of the following pairs of sentences into a single sentence by turning one of them into a subordinate clause. Use a subordinating conjunction that makes sense with the two sentences. Add a comma if the subordinate clause is at the beginning of the sentence.

EXAMPLE

Although d

ˆDoctors can attempt to predict a pregnant woman's delivery

b

date/,ˆBabies keep their own schedules.

1. The TV news recently reported that Jahmal Haney delivered his first baby. He was only eight years old.

2. Jahmal's mother, Donna Murray, wasn't due for another month. She started having contractions in the middle of the night.

3. Two hours later, she called 911. She realized she wasn't going to make it to the hospital.

4. The 911 operator, Sean Stentiford, asked Murray if there was anyone else at home. She handed the phone to her son.

5. His mother went to lie down in the bedroom. Jahmal listened carefully to Stentiford's instructions.

6. Stentiford told Jahmal to make sure his mother was lying in the middle of the bed. They didn't want the baby to fall on the floor.

7. Jahmal returned from the bedroom. He told Stentiford he could see the baby's head.

8. Stentiford instructed Jahmal to put his hands under the head. His mother pushed the baby out.

9. Jahmal had to run back and forth between his mother in the bedroom and the phone in the living room. He helped deliver his new baby sister, Samantha Elise Murray.

10. The ambulance arrived. The baby had already been born.

Chapter 28: Parallelism

28-1: Correcting Errors in Parallelism (1)

Edit the following sentences to make them parallel.

EXAMPLE

and performance

Consumers should get information on the price ⌃ of a product ~~and how well it performs~~ before making a purchase.

1. Among college students, halogen lamps have become more popular than using a traditional incandescent lamp.

2. Halogen lamps are more popular because they are cheaper and the light they produce is brighter.

3. However, there are two problems with halogen lamps: They not only cause fires but also lots of energy is used.

4. A 300-watt halogen bulb gets almost three times as hot as to use a 150-watt incandescent bulb.

5. A Harvard engineering professor discovered that halogen lamps—not toasters, hair dryers, stereos, refrigerators, or the use of computers—were responsible for rising energy consumption in residence halls.

6. Some colleges are considering both banning halogen lamps in dormitories and to offer students low-energy fluorescent lamps.

7. The new lamps would be provided either free or they would be at a discount.

8. These energy-efficient lamps cost about four to five times more than the price of halogen lamps.

9. Unfortunately, most consumers would rather save money when they buy an item than when using it.

10. To figure out a lamp's lifetime cost, you have to consider the cost of the lamp itself, of replacement bulbs, and the price of using electricity.

28-2: Correcting Errors in Parallelism (2)

Edit the following sentences to make them parallel.

EXAMPLE

What people who suffer from chronic medical problems need most

coworkers

from family, friends, ~~and those they work with~~ are compassion and
⌃

support.

1. A migraine is an intense headache characterized by pulsing pain, nausea, dizziness, double vision, and by being sensitive to light and sound.

2. Migraines are often triggered by red wine, chocolate, aged cheese, and by cured meats.

3. These terrible headaches can also be triggered by certain medicines and when you eat certain food additives.

4. Migraines are three times more common in women than men have them.

5. Women's migraines are often hormonal, related to the fluctuation of both estrogen and of progesterone during their menstrual cycles.

6. Birth control pills or taking estrogen replacement therapy can make hormonal migraines much worse.

7. Throughout history, there have been many failed remedies for migraines, such as purging, bleeding, encircling the head with a hangman's noose, and to drill a hole in the skull.

8. In a famous essay entitled "In Bed," the writer Joan Didion argues that people with migraines not only suffer from the headaches themselves but also the common belief that they are somehow causing their own sickness.

9. Despite what some people think, migraines are caused neither by having a bad attitude nor because you have a certain personality trait.

10. An international team of scientists has not only isolated the gene that causes one severe type of migraine, but also they expect to find genes for more common forms.

Chapter 29: Sentence Variety

29-1: Starting Sentences with an Adverb

Edit the following sentences to begin with an adverb. You may need to add an adverb if an appropriate adverb is not already in the sentence.

EXAMPLE

Usually, it
~~It usually~~ takes people a long time to grieve the loss of a loved one.

1. My friend recently has had problems concentrating and finishing the projects she starts.

2. Very thorough, Karen says she has felt distracted since her brother died of cancer last spring.

3. This has gotten in her way at work, where she is expected to complete assignments on time.

4. Her boss is very understanding and told Karen that she would like to support her through this difficult time.

5. Karen went to a psychologist to see if there was anything that Karen could do about her concentration problems.

6. The psychologist explained that the overwhelming emotions Karen was experiencing were completely normal after the loss of a loved one.

7. "These feelings do not last forever," the psychologist explained, "and the grief will eventually become less consuming."

8. After talking with the psychologist, Karen began to attend a support group for people who have lost relatives to cancer.

9. Karen said she began to feel a little better very soon after joining the group.

10. She is getting back on her feet.

29-2: Joining Ideas Using an *-ing* Verb Form

Edit the following pairs of sentences by joining them with an *-ing* verb form.

EXAMPLE

Wanting   *many young people*

~~Many young people want~~ to stay in touch with friends/ ~~They~~ send

a nearly constant stream of instant messages.

1. My daughter types text messages on her cell phone. She chats with her friends throughout the day.

2. She understands that I am unfamiliar with this technology. She showed me how it works.

3. She said that people use abbreviated phrases, like "How RU?" in messages. They can send and receive notes quickly.

4. I felt behind the times when I heard this. I asked my daughter, "Does everyone understand all the abbreviations?"

5. My daughter laughed. She said, "Not all the abbreviations, but you catch on over time."

6. She hoped I would catch on, too. She typed "Sup" into her cell phone and handed it to me.

7. She watched me closely. She asked, "What do you think that means?"

8. I shook my head. I said, "I haven't a clue."

9. She threw her head back. She yelled, "What's up?"

10. I wagged my finger. I replied, not entirely as a joke, "You better not use that kind of language in your English papers."

29-3: Joining Ideas Using an *-ed* Verb Form

Join the following pairs of sentences by using an *-ed* verb.

EXAMPLE

~~The great novel *Moby-Dick* was~~ b̂ased partly on the true story of
Moby-Dick
the *Essex*/ ̂It̂ is a tale of a man's obsession with a white whale.

1. The *Essex* was an old whaling ship by the time it sailed its last voyage in 1820. It was regarded as particularly lucky.

2. The *Essex* inspired the final scene of Herman Melville's *Moby-Dick*. The *Essex* was attacked by a sperm whale.

3. The larger story actually began after the ship was sunk. It was passed down over the years through town lore.

4. Nantucket, home of the *Essex,* was a prosperous whaling town. It was considered enlightened and a good place for free blacks to live during the era of slavery.

5. Many of the sailors on the *Essex* were only fifteen years old. They were orphaned and desperate for work.

6. Thomas Nickerson was a fourteen-year-old cabin boy. He was determined to record what happened during the attack and in the ninety days that followed.

7. Nickerson's narrative recorded starvation, madness, and desperation. It was discovered in 1981.

8. Twenty crew members were stranded on small boats for ninety days after the *Essex* was sunk. They were forced to resort to desperate measures to stay alive.

9. Melville's narrator, Ishmael, was troubled by his captain's obsession. His story ends when the boat sinks.

10. The crew of the *Essex* may have wished for that fate by the end of their ordeal. They were starved and driven to desperate measures.

29-4: Joining Ideas Using an Appositive

Join the following pairs of sentences by using an appositive.

EXAMPLE

, a brave group of people,
Health-care professionals˄have high-stress jobs. ~~They are a brave group of people.~~

1. My brother has some very interesting stories from his work. He is a paramedic.

2. Rush hour afforded him a particularly good story last week. Rush hour is a tense and hectic time for ambulance workers.

3. A pregnant woman called from her car phone. The woman was a rush hour victim.

4. The woman had started to go into labor. Labor is one of the most intense experiences a person can have.

5. The woman hoped that an ambulance could rescue her from the traffic jam. She was a first-time mother.

6. Jake was working with my brother that day. Jake is one of the best ambulance drivers in the area.

7. They found the woman about an eighth of a mile down the highway from where she had called. The woman was a model of courage despite her pain and fear.

8. They left her car at the side of the road. Her car was a 2005 red Lexus.

9. They lifted her into the ambulance and sped away. The ambulance was a godsend to the woman and her unborn child.

10. The woman gave birth to her child 7 minutes after arriving at the hospital. Her child was a healthy little girl.

29-5: Joining Ideas with an Adjective Clause

Combine the following pairs of sentences by using an adjective clause that begins with *who, which,* or *that.*

EXAMPLE

Hummus is a healthful food made from chick peas./ ~~It~~ can be used as a spread for pita bread.
(that inserted above)

1. Alice Waters is a well-known chef. She has helped bring attention to organic produce and locally grown foods.

2. Waters has a restaurant named Chez Panisse. It is located in Berkeley, California.

3. Chez Panisse uses only locally grown foods. These foods are pesticide- and chemical-free.

4. In recent years, many people have become much more aware of the quality of the foods they eat. They have heard or read about the organic farm movement.

5. They have come to realize that the nutritional value of food involves many factors. It is usually associated only with vitamin content.

6. Organic produce has to be sold more quickly and is therefore fresher. It often has a higher vitamin content.

7. In addition, organic produce is free of pesticides and chemicals. Pesticides and chemicals can be carcinogenic.

8. Chemicals can have other effects. These effects may be less dangerous but are still undesirable.

9. For example, sulfites can produce an allergic reaction in many people. Sulfites are often added to fruits and vegetables to prevent discoloration.

10. Adding sulfites to fruits and vegetables also makes them appear fresher for longer. This allows fruits and vegetables to be sold several weeks after they have been picked.

29-6: Improving Sentence Variety

Edit the following sentences or pairs of sentences to create better sentence variety. Use the techniques covered in this chapter: starting a sentence with an *-ly* adverb or joining sentences by using an *-ing* word, *-ed* word, appositive, or adjective clause that begins with *who, which,* or *that.* In many cases, there is more than one way to combine the sentences.

EXAMPLE

Frequently, p

~~P~~regnant women who smoke in public are ~~frequently~~ criticized by complete strangers.

1. A group of scientists recently discovered that babies whose mothers smoked during pregnancy have the same levels of nicotine in their bodies as adult smokers.

2. The results of their study strongly suggest that these newborns go through withdrawal. The study was presented at a meeting of the American College of Cardiology.

3. Dr. Claude Hanet said that the baby of a smoking mother should be considered an ex-smoker. Dr. Hanet spoke at the conference.

4. The study examined the urine of 273 babies and toddlers. The study was conducted by a team of Belgian researchers.

5. Of these children, 139 were newborns. These newborns were one to three days old.

6. Researchers checked the children's urine for cotinine. Cotinine is the substance that remains in the body for several days after nicotine breaks down.

7. Some of the mothers had smoked during pregnancy. They had newborns with cotinine levels that were about the same as their own.

8. In toddlers with smoking mothers, cotinine levels were significantly higher than in certain adult nonsmokers. These adults were exposed to secondhand smoke at home.

9. Pregnant women should not only quit smoking but also avoid secondhand smoke. Secondhand smoke is smoke inhaled from other people's cigarettes.

10. Studies have found that even nonsmoking pregnant women can pass cancer-causing chemicals to their fetuses. These nonsmokers have inhaled secondhand smoke.

Chapter 30: Formal English and ESL Concerns

30-1: Editing Various ESL Errors (1)

Edit the following sentences for ESL errors.

EXAMPLE

According to the Library of Congress's *Poetry* Web site, ~~a~~ *the* main

duty of the U.S. poet laureate is to increase our nation's appreciation

of poetry.

1. The poet laureate is the appointed position.

2. The Library of Congress an American poet to serve annually chooses.

3. Ted Kooser was named poet laureate in 2004, and him is well known for writing poetry while working at a life-insurance company.

4. Have you ever hear of him?

5. Kooser he created the "American Life in Poetry" program.

6. Provides a weekly poetry column to newspapers around the country.

7. Newspapers that are interested on poetry can run the column for free.

8. Also, subscribers will can read a new poem every week.

9. Each poet laureate has contribute different ideas to the program.

10. To find up more about past poet laureates, visit the Library of Congress Web site.

30-2: Editing Various ESL Errors (2)

Edit the following sentences for ESL errors.

EXAMPLE

Are you aware <del>at</del> *of* the term "super foods"?

1. In recent years, you had probably seen many articles written about the healing power of certain foods.

2. Blueberries, for example, fiber and vitamin C contain.

3. Omega-3 fats help in the fight about heart disease.

4. Salmon and walnuts are two foods that contain they.

5. Heart disease is the number one killer of women in America, but might become less of a threat if diets are improved.

6. Beans, especially soybeans, might can prevent heart disease and some types of cancer.

7. In the Middle East, dates have been praised for thousands of the years.

8. Dried fruit, like dates, does not requires refrigeration and contains many vitamins and minerals.

9. Some people refuse eating fruit, fish, and nuts because they don't like the taste.

10. However, if you are try to stay healthy, eating right is essential.

Chapter 31: Word Choice

31-1: Improving Word Choice

Rewrite the following sentences to eliminate the four language problems covered in Chapter 31: vague and abstract words, slang, wordiness, and clichés.

EXAMPLE

Graphic design is a way cool thing to do because it's fun and you can earn a lot of dough performing it because it pays great.

Graphic design is an excellent career; it's fun, and it also pays well.

1. I am writing you this letter to let you know how totally awesome it was to meet you the other day at the interview I had with you.

2. I also wanted to take this opportunity to thank you after the fact for taking the time out of your busy day to interview me for the job at your company.

3. As far as I'm concerned, Nadler & Lattimore seems like a wicked cool place to work, and the job seems truly mint and right up my alley.

4. I have to say that I think I have good qualifications for the job in question, due to the fact that I have taken some courses in graphic design and advertising.

5. Based on the description you were kind enough to give me pertaining to the position, I know that I could perform at an unbelievable level as a summer intern, leaving no stone unturned in the performance of my duties and responsibilities.

6. I think it is fair to say that for me, the job would be nothing less than the opportunity of a lifetime, a dream come true—which is what I told you already at the interview.

(continued)

7. I also wanted to inform you that I have made phone contact with all the folks I gave you as references, just to let them know that you might be calling them sometime in the foreseeable future to check me out, so to speak.

_____

8. Please do not wait to let me know if it turns out that you have any other questions pertaining to my experience and background.

_____

9. As for me, I'll just be chillin' as I wait to hear from you about whether or not you decided that I'm your man.

_____

10. Once again, it was nice of you to interview me, and I thank you for your time from the bottom of my heart.

_____

Chapter 32: Commonly Confused Words

32-1: Using the Right Word (1)

In the following sentences, underline the correct word from the choices in parentheses.

EXAMPLE

Parents have to decide what is (<u>right</u>, write) for their children because adults know better (<u>than</u>, then) kids do.

1. I need some good (advice, advise), so I thought I would (right, write) you this letter.

2. When I'm feeling confused, (its, it's) often helpful for me to put my thoughts down on a (peace, piece) of paper.

3. I really don't have anyone else I can turn to (accept, except) my sister, (who's, whose) children (are, our) much older (than, then) mine.

4. But in the (passed, past), she and I have often disagreed on how to raise (are, our) kids, so I don't think she's the (right, write) person to (advice, advise) me this time.

5. My problem is that (their, there, they're) is a girl in my daughter's first-grade class (who's, whose) always inviting Anna over (to, too, two) play.

6. Anna (use, used) to play with Kate, but (than, then) she told me that she really didn't want to anymore, either at (are, our) apartment or at (their, there, they're) house.

7. I believe in the (principal, principle) that you should (of, have) the (right, write) to decide who (your, you're) friends (are, our)—even if (your, you're) only seven.

8. So I don't think (its, it's) fair to force my daughter to play with Kate, whether or not I understand or approve (of, have) Anna's reasons for disliking her.

9. However, my (conscience, conscious) is bothered by deception, (to, too), particularly when I'm the one (who's, whose) doing the deceiving.

10. I (know, no) I'll never (have, of) any (piece, peace) (have, of) mind until I (quiet, quit, quite) lying (to, too) Kate's mother, Diane.

11. Well, maybe (its, it's) not (quite, quiet) lying, but I (use, used) to make up phony excuses for Anna whenever Diane called.

12. I kept saying Anna was busy or sick, instead (have, of) just sitting down with Diane (an, and) telling her the unpleasant truth.

(continued)

13. At first, I wasn't really (conscience, conscious) that I was misleading her, because the situation was so (knew, new).

14. I guess I was simply trying to (by, buy) some time, hoping I could persuade Anna (to, too, two) change her (mine, mind).

15. (Than, Then) I'd find myself getting annoyed with Diane for not taking the hint, even (though, through) I (knew, new) I was giving her mixed signals.

16. I was trying (to, too, two) avoid having (a, an) awkward conversation vaguely agreeing that the (to, too, two) girls would get together some other time.

17. When Diane calls again, I definitely don't want to (accept, except) another invitation, but I also don't want to hurt her feelings or (loose, lose) her friendship.

18. I should (have, of) just been honest with her from the very beginning, but I guess I was afraid (have, of) how the truth would (affect, effect) her—(an, and) Kate (to, too).

19. I thought it would be kinder to tell (a, an) little white lie (than, then) to come (right, write) out (an, and) say, "My daughter doesn't like (your, you're) daughter."

20. I (suppose, supposed) that I should try to (fine, find) a good time to (set, sit) down with Diane (an, and) tell her the truth.

32-2: Using the Right Word (2)

In the following sentences, correct any words that are used incorrectly. Some sentences may contain more than one error.

EXAMPLE

Sometimes, ~~their~~ *there* are things about ~~you're~~ *your* friends that you have to simply ~~except~~ *accept*.

1. Do you no anyone whose always giving you advise whether your asking for it or not?

2. I use to be friends with someone like that, an I just accepted the situation.

3. Elena thought she had the write to tell me what to do about everything, and that was the basis of are relationship.

4. We would be talking about something going on in my life, but than she would interrupt me too start talking about her own supposedly similar experience.

5. One time when we were on the phone, I counted twenty-to times that Elena cut me off before I was threw with my sentence.

6. She probably wasn't conscience of what she was doing, or of the affect her behavior was having on me, but buy the end of the conversation, I could of screamed.

7. I suddenly realized that Elena wasn't listening to me; she was simply waiting to talk about herself or to offer me her next peace of unwelcome advice.

8. Their is only so much of that kind of "friendship" I can except—it's just not worth the trouble.

9. Though eventually I quit talking to Elena about anything except her new boyfriend, she never even noticed how quite I had become during are conversations.

10. Then, I started thinking about how it would feel to loose Elena's friendship, and I suddenly new that I wouldn't mine at all.

Chapter 33: Spelling

33-1: Using the Six Spelling Rules (1)

In the following sentences, choose the correct spelling from the choices in parentheses. You may want to refer to the six spelling rules explained in Chapter 33.

EXAMPLE

Sometimes, I have trouble in school because I act a little too (<u>conceited</u>, concieted) in class.

1. I (believe, beleive) I did well on the English paper I wrote last week.

2. I'm (assumeing, assuming) that I didn't make any spelling mistakes, even though I was (hurrying, hurriing) to turn it in on time.

3. (Luckily, Luckyly), my girlfriend proofread a rough draft and caught a few errors that I then (corrected, correctted) in my final version.

4. I had (omited, omitted) the letter e in forming the plural of the word potato, and I had (flipped, fliped) the letters e and i in the word (acheive, achieve).

5. Until I started checking everything in the dictionary, I (useed, used) to be so (worried, worryed) whenever I (submited, submitted) an assignment.

6. My papers always came back from the teacher with comments (saing, saying) that (sloppyness, sloppiness) was my main problem.

7. My teacher, Professor Bauer, grades us based on our writing (portfolios, portfolioes), and she expects to see a lot of (improvment, improvement) during the semester.

8. She doesn't care if you wear a nose ring or are covered with (tattoos, tatooes)—she just can't stand (laziness, lazyness).

9. I can't (concieve, conceive) of a more (encourageing, encouraging) teacher than Professor Bauer, and I'm (hopeful, hopful) that I'll be able to take another class with her.

10. This year at graduation, she (clapped, claped) and (cheerred, cheered) when two of her former students gave (speeches, speechs).

33-2: Using the Six Spelling Rules (2)

In the following sentences, correct any misspelled words. You may want to refer to the six spelling rules in Chapter 33.

EXAMPLE

When my sister got her own apartment and moved out of the house,
begged
I beged my mother to let me get a cat.
^

1. My sister is allergic to cats and to dogs, so we definitly could not get a cat while she lived at home.

2. Since she moved out, I've been convinceing my mother that we should get a cat.

3. When I first brought up the subject, my mother said that she prefered dogs to cats.

4. Since I don't like dogs very much, I couldn't beleive my ears.

5. Dogs are far more troublsome than cats, I told her.

6. Cats are also much cleanner animals than dogs.

7. I tried to persuade my mother that she would be much happyer if she didn't have to get up early every day to walk a dog.

8. When I get home from class and then have to go right to work, I know that I won't feel like offerring to walk a dog.

9. I reminded her of how our nieghbor's dog barks every night and keeps everyone awake.

10. Eventually, my mother said that we didn't really need to have an arguement—she wanted a cat all along!

33-3: Using the Six Spelling Rules (3)

In the following sentences, correct any misspelled words. You may refer to the six spelling rules in Chapter 33.

EXAMPLE

My mother and I decided to get a cat, but ~~niether~~ *neither* of us wanted to buy one from a pet store.

1. Both my mother and I had heard storys about pet stores mistreating animals.

2. Besides, we both knew that we could not afford thier prices.

3. There are lots of animal shelteres that rescue abandoned and unwanted animals.

4. By making a donation to the shelter, you can adopt one of these animals, which might otherwise be put to sleep.

5. My mother and I scheduleed a time to visit the shelters together.

6. We both were hopeing to find a kitten.

7. As soon as we entered the first shelter, however, I spotted a big, fluffy, adult gray cat.

8. I don't know what happened, but I just knew that he was the cat I wanted.

9. We were able to take him out of his cage, and we found that he was very freindly.

10. My mother admited that she too had immediately chosen that cat, so we adopted him and brought him home.

33-4: Correcting Spelling Mistakes (1)

In the following sentences, find and correct any spelling mistakes. You may want to refer to the list of commonly misspelled words in Chapter 33.

EXAMPLE

> usually   their   business
> My parents ~~usualy~~ mind ~~there~~ own ~~busness~~ and let me make my own
> decisions—but not always.

1. During my sophmore year in college, I decided that I wanted to become a high school mathematics teacher.

2. My carreer choice definately came as a great surprize to my parents and freinds, and it has caused alot of arguements.

3. My father was incredably dissappointed that I didn't want to go into the family busness—a jewlry store.

4. My mother probly assumed that I would become a secretery or work in a conveneince store untill I got marryed and had kids.

5. In my opinion, my parents have never shown much confidence in my inteligence or judgment.

6. As a child, I never recieved any encouragment for my schoolwork, since I was percieved as a good athleet but a poor student.

7. I was especialy aweful at arithemetic, and by the second grade, I allready felt anxious and embarassed every time I had to anser a question in class.

8. By the eighth grade, I was convinced that I would never acheive anything in life—that I was just not maent to suceed.

9. All that changed when I got to college and finally began to analize my strengths and intrests in a supportive envirment.

10. My adviser doesn't think it's wierd that I want to pursue a job in teaching; in fact, she sincerely believes that I will be an excellant role model for kids who have had similar school experiences.

33-5: Correcting Spelling Mistakes (2)

In the following sentences, correct any misspelled words. You may want to refer to the six spelling rules and the list of commonly misspelled words in Chapter 33.

EXAMPLE

My mother and I were both happy with our new cat, but we were

surprised

~~surprized~~ to find that we could not stop thinking about the other
　　^

animals we had seen in the shelter.

1. Untill we had gone to the shelter to adopt a cat, niether of us had thought much about how many abandoned and stray animals there are in the city.

2. I tryed to discribe to my sister how sad some of the animals in the shelter looked that day.

3. I am sure that animals can feel sadness and lonelyness the same way people do.

4. As soon as we saw how quickly and happyly our cat, Fluffy Gus, made himself at home, I regreted that we hadn't adopted another animal as well.

5. I didn't want my mother to think I was disapointed with our new cat, so I didn't mention my feelings to her.

6. About a week after we got the cat, my mother told me that it was neccessary for us too go back to the shelter.

7. I became worryed thinking that somthing was wrong with Fluffy Gus.

8. The cat was fine, but my mother had allready decided that we should adopt a dog from the shelter, too.

9. So we went back to the shelter, and we came home with the prettyest little black and white mutt.

10. The dog and the cat imediately became friends—but know my mother and I have to agree on a name for the dog.

Chapter 34: Commas

34-1: Using Commas in a Series

In the following sentences, add commas where they are needed in the series. If a sentence is already correct, write **OK** next to it.

EXAMPLE

Babysitting a newborn can be fun, enlightening, and exhausting.

1. Studies show that newborn babies immediately begin to explore their environment by using their senses of sight hearing touch smell and taste.

2. Yet, it is difficult to tell what newborns can perceive because they are often sleeping dozing or crying.

3. Researchers test what newborns can see by showing them objects or pictures and then observing their responses.

4. They film their eye movements and measure changes in their heart rates sucking and sweating.

5. Research has shown that newborns can see large objects that are close to them but not small objects that are far away.

6. A newborn sees poorly because its brain eyes and nerves have not yet fully developed.

7. At first, infants can focus only on lines corners and the edges of objects.

8. Patterns with large shapes clear outlines and high contrast are what they see best.

9. Every parent grandparent or babysitter knows that infants love to look at people's faces.

10. In one study, babies as young as an hour old could tell the difference between a simple drawing of a face and several other patterns.

34-2: Using Commas in a Compound Sentence

In the following compound sentences, add commas where they are needed.

EXAMPLE

A strong desire to succeed can take you far, but it can also cause you a lot of stress.

1. Some people are more motivated to achieve excellence than other people so psychologists are interested in understanding why.

2. People with high achievement motivation have a strong desire to master tasks and they experience great satisfaction when they achieve success.

3. In one experiment, researchers gave children a test designed to measure their need for achievement and then they asked these children to play a ring-toss game.

4. Those children who had scored low on the test stood so close to the target that they always scored or they stood so far away that they always missed.

5. In other words, they succeeded at an unchallenging task or they failed at an impossible one.

6. In contrast, the children who had scored well on the test stood far enough away from the target to make the game challenging but they did not stand so far away as to guarantee their own failure.

7. Psychologists believe that people with high achievement motivation tend to set challenging but realistic goals for themselves and they are willing to take risks to achieve those goals.

8. They experience intense satisfaction from success but they are not discouraged by failure if they feel they have tried their best.

9. People with low achievement motivation also prefer success to failure but they usually experience relief at *not* having failed rather than pleasure or pride at having succeeded.

10. They do not tend to seek out feedback from critics nor do they struggle with a problem instead of quitting in the face of failure.

34-3: Using Commas after Introductory Word Groups

In the following sentences, add commas where they are needed after introductory words or word groups.

EXAMPLE

Within the past few years, the issue of violence on television has come

to be recognized as a serious problem.

1. According to a recent study children can unlearn violent behavior in less than six months.

2. Published in *The Journal of the American Medical Association* the study helps disprove the idea that nothing can be done to stop violence among America's youth.

3. For Americans between the ages of fifteen and twenty-four violence is one of the leading causes of death.

4. Financed by the Centers for Disease Control and Prevention the study involved 790 second- and third-graders at twelve schools in the state of Washington.

5. Over a period of sixteen to twenty weeks about half of these students were taught a violence-prevention curriculum.

6. During the study the behavior of this group of students was compared with the behavior of the students who did not take the course.

7. Six months after the program ended students who had taken the course engaged in about thirty fewer aggressive acts per day at school than the students in the other group.

8. Significantly aggressive behavior (such as hitting, kicking, and shoving) increased in those children who did not take the course.

9. Developed by a Seattle educator the Second Step antiviolence program consists of weekly or twice-weekly sessions lasting about half an hour each.

10. Widely used in American and Canadian schools the program is designed to teach empathy, problem solving, and anger management to preschool through ninth-grade students.

34-4: Using Commas to Set Off Appositives and Interrupters

In the following sentences, add commas where they are needed to set off appositives and interrupters.

EXAMPLE

The exploration of outer space, once strongly supported by the public,

is now less important to the average person.

1. Thousands of "snowballs" from outer space are hitting Earth's atmosphere every day according to scientists at a recent meeting of the American Geophysical Union in Baltimore.

2. Over billions of years they reported this bombardment of cosmic slush has added vast amounts of water to Earth's atmosphere and oceans.

3. These extraterrestrial snowballs made up of ice and cosmic dust may have played a key role in nurturing life on this planet and perhaps elsewhere in the solar system.

4. They are about forty feet in diameter the size of a small house.

5. These small, cometlike objects unlike large comets are extremely hard to see because they break up into fragments and then vaporize.

6. Astronomers and physicists however have speculated about their existence since 1986.

7. Dr. Louis A. Frank a physicist at the University of Iowa first theorized about them to explain the dark spots he observed in images of Earth's sunlit atmosphere.

8. Dr. Frank noticed these spots or atmospheric holes while analyzing data from NASA's *Dynamics Explorer 1* satellite.

9. NASA's *Polar* satellite a veteran space explorer produced more detailed images of these atmospheric holes.

10. Many scientists now believe that these snowballs are hitting Earth's outer atmosphere at an incredible rate of five to thirty a minute or up to 43,000 a day.

34-5: Using Commas with Adjective Clauses

In the following sentences, add commas around or before adjective clauses where they are needed. Remember that if the adjective clause is essential to the meaning of the sentence, you should not use commas. Some sentences may contain more than one adjective clause. If a sentence is already correct, write **OK** next to it.

EXAMPLE

Many writers use their own experiences as the basis for their works,

which can then reveal a lot about the author's life.

1. Bernard Malamud who was born in Brooklyn in 1914 wrote novels and short stories about Jewish immigrant life.

2. His parents who were Russian immigrants owned a struggling neighborhood grocery store.

3. In fact, the grocer character who appears in several of Malamud's works was modeled after his own father.

4. A baseball player who is endowed with supernatural abilities is the hero of Malamud's first novel.

5. *The Natural* which was made into a movie starring Robert Redford is considered one of the greatest baseball novels of all time.

6. Malamud's first short-story collection which won the National Book Award is called *The Magic Barrel*.

7. In the title story, a young man who is studying to become a rabbi falls in love with a woman who turns out to be his marriage broker's daughter.

8. The novel that earned Malamud both the National Book Award and the Pulitzer Prize is *The Fixer*.

9. This novel which is set in Russia is about a Jewish handyman who is falsely accused of ritual murder.

10. Malamud who died in 1986 is considered one of the greatest contemporary American fiction writers.

34-6: Using Commas in Other Situations

In the following sentences, add commas where they are needed. If a sentence is already correct, write **OK** next to it.

EXAMPLE

Even when I think one of my relatives is making the wrong choice,

I often say, "It's your decision," because none of them ever listens to me.

1. Two years ago, my parents decided to sell their house in St. Paul Minnesota and retire to Florida.

2. During a vacation they had stopped in Lake Worth, Florida to visit my father's cousin Lila, and they decided they liked the area.

3. On December 29 2004 my mother called to tell me that they had put down a deposit on a house that was going to be built in a new development near Lila's condominium.

4. When I heard the news, I said "Mom have you and Dad gone out of your minds? Isn't this kind of sudden?"

5. "Yes it is" she replied "but I think your father and I have made a wise decision."

6. Both my parents have always insisted that they would never retire to a place like Florida or Phoenix Arizona, because they enjoy the winter.

7. My father grew up in Madison Wisconsin and moved to St. Paul in 1952.

8. My mother grew up in Minneapolis and moved to St. Paul when she married my father in June 1958.

9. "Peter we're putting the Carter Avenue house on the market this May," my mother calmly informed me, "and we expect to be moving to Florida by September or October 2005."

10. On October 3 2005 my parents moved to a small stucco house at 61 Rosewood Lane Green Acres Florida 33463.

Chapter 35: Apostrophes

35-1: Using Apostrophes to Show Ownership

Edit the following sentences by adding apostrophes where they are needed to show ownership and by crossing out any apostrophes that are used incorrectly or positioned incorrectly in the word.

EXAMPLE

Animal rights is a big issue among students in my state's high

school's.

1. There is a growing rebellion in the nations high school's against dissecting animals in biology class.

2. More and more students' feel that dissection is inhumane and unnecessary.

3. Until recently, a students' refusal to dissect has usually resulted in a lower grade or other academic penalty.

4. However, California, Florida, Maryland, New York, and Pennsylvania have passed laws' that allow students to complete alternative science assignments if they oppose dissection.

5. Other states' are considering legislation modeled on these states laws.

6. In California, it was fifteen-year-old Jennifer Grahams refusal to dissect a frog that caused her state's lawmakers to debate the issue.

7. When Grahams school would not allow her to complete an alternative assignment, she sued the school district over it's policy.

8. The California courts ruling stated that schools could require students to dissect a frog, but only if it's death was from natural causes.

9. Grahams lawsuit led state lawmakers in California to pass the nations first laws protecting students who oppose dissection.

10. Because Jasmine Dixons reasons for opposing dissection are environmental as well as humanitarian, her Indianapolis high school is allowing her to fulfill her' science requirement by taking an environmental class instead of biology.

35-2: Using Apostrophes in Contractions and with Letters and Time

Edit the following sentences by adding apostrophes where they are needed and by crossing out any apostrophes that are used incorrectly or positioned incorrectly in the word.

EXAMPLE

My older sister said she'll try to come to my graduation ceremony, but

I'm not sure if she can really make it in time.

1. At last years graduation ceremony, I could'nt believe how long it took to hand out all the diplomas.

2. I wasnt surprised that the president of the college called the graduating students' up to the stage according to the first letter of their last names.

3. But I would'nt have guessed that it would take half an hour' for just the *A*s, *B*s, *C*s, and *D*s to get their diplomas.

4. Sitting in the hot sun, I started to realize that it would take about two hour's time to get through the rest of the alphabet.

5. For some letters, student's were filing up to the stage by the 20s and 30s, but for the *Q*s, *X*s, and *Z*s, students were going up in 2s and 3s.

6. I think its going to take even longer to hand out diplomas to this years' graduating class, but well find out in a weeks' time.

7. Im pretty sure that the Class of 2006 has about fifty more students than the Class of 2005, and it's members are more diverse in age and ethnic background.

8. Ive heard that lots of students are planning to wear 06s all over their caps and gowns.

9. My parents sent me an enormous graduation card covered with *X*s and *O*s; my boyfriend didnt know that its customary to use those letters to stand for kisses and hugs.

10. Its hard to believe that in a few month's time, I'll be a college graduate starting my new job as a teachers aide.

Chapter 36: Quotation Marks

36-1: Punctuating Direct and Indirect Quotations

Edit the following sentences by adding quotation marks and commas where they are needed and by crossing out quotation marks and commas that are used incorrectly. Also, correct any other punctuation mistakes you notice. If a sentence is already correct, write **OK** next to it.

EXAMPLE

"They are too dangerous" I said when my brother told me that he

wants to get a motorcycle.

1. Darryl called his parents from the hospital emergency room to tell them that, "he had just been in an accident."

2. I was riding my bike down New Scotland Avenue, he explained when his mother picked up the phone. A guy who had just parked his van in front of the Bagel Baron opened his door.

3. Darryl told his mother that he had hit the door of the van and gone flying off his bicycle.

4. "Luckily, I was wearing a helmet, he said or I'd probably be dead."

5. Are you all right"? interrupted Darryl's mother. "What hospital are you at"?

6. "I hurt my shoulder, but I'm not sure how badly because I haven't seen a doctor yet." replied Darryl. "I'm at St. Peter's.

7. "George" his mother called to his father, pick up the phone in the kitchen. Darryl hurt his shoulder in a bicycle accident."

8. Darryl said, he had to get off the phone because the doctor was ready to examine him.

9. "Okay, honey," said his mother. She assured him that they would be at the hospital in ten minutes.

10. Don't let them do anything to you until we get there and talk to the doctor! insisted Darryl's father.

36-2: Using Quotation Marks for Direct Quotations and Certain Titles

Edit the following sentences by adding quotation marks and commas where they are needed around direct quotations and titles and by crossing out quotation marks and commas that are used incorrectly.

EXAMPLE

Whenever someone asks me which poets I like, I tell them that "Anne

Sexton is my favorite."

1. I think you would enjoy reading some poems by Martín Espada, my English teacher told me during our conference.

2. I'm going to lend you a book called *City of Coughing and Dead Radiators* she said.

3. "I'll take a look," I replied but I really don't like poetry very much."

4. I had a student last year who announced, I hate poetry, but he changed his mind after reading this book, replied my teacher.

5. A week later I told Professor Macarrulla that "I too had changed my mind about poetry after reading Espada's book."

6. Which poems did you like the best? Professor Macarrulla asked me.

7. I told her that my favorites were, Borofels and Day of the Dead on Wortman Avenue.

8. I explained that "Borofels reminded me of my own experience growing up in Brooklyn with Puerto Rican parents who spoke very little English."

9. Professor Macarrulla said that her favorite poem in the book was, Who Burns for the Perfection of Paper.

10. "I like that poem, she explained because it reminds me that no matter how much success you achieve in life, you should never forget your working-class roots.

Chapter 37: Other Punctuation

37-1: Using Colons, Semicolons, Parentheses, Dashes, and Hyphens (1)

Edit the following sentences by adding colons, semicolons, parentheses, dashes, and hyphens where needed. You may also need to change some commas to semicolons.

EXAMPLE

Chemistry‸the subject I almost failed in high school‸has always fascinated me.

1. Scientists at Cornell University have discovered something that seems too good to be true a strain of bacteria that can break down some of the most toxic chemicals in polluted water.

2. Dr. Stephen H. Zinder and his colleagues have found this pollution fighting organism in sewage sludge the solid matter produced during sewage treatment.

3. This strain of bacteria breaks down two of the most common pollutants of groundwater the chemical compounds trichloroethene and tetrachloroethene.

4. Both chlorinated compounds are solvents that are used in such products as glue, paint remover, and cleaning solutions for clothing, machinery, brakes, engines, and electronic parts.

5. These two water polluting solvents can damage the human nervous system they are also suspected carcinogens cancer causing substances.

6. They are major groundwater pollutants because for years they were handled carelessly spilled on the ground, poured down drains, and dumped into landfills before their danger was clearly understood.

7. These solvents seep hundreds of feet into the earth and then dissolve gradually as groundwater the main source of drinking water for half the U.S. population flows by.

8. Scientists have known for about fifteen years that bacteria can sometimes change these chlorinated compounds into ethylene the harmless gas that causes fruit to ripen.

9. However, the exact chemical process as well as the conditions necessary for it to occur have been poorly understood until now.

10. The Cornell scientists have figured out that these bacteria break down the solvents by using them the way people use oxygen for the cycle of biochemical reactions known as respiration breathing.

37-2: Using Colons, Semicolons, Parentheses, Dashes, and Hyphens (2)

Edit the following sentences by adding colons, semicolons, parentheses, dashes, and hyphens or by correcting errors in their usage. If a sentence is already correct, write **OK** next to it.

EXAMPLE

There have recently been many movies adapted from classic works

of literature*/* *Sense and Sensibility, The Scarlet Letter, The Crucible,* and

Portrait of a Lady.

1. The 1993 movie *Schindler's List* directed by Steven Spielberg won the Academy Award for Best Picture in 1994.

2. The movie tells the true story of an unlikely hero of the Holocaust; a German factory owner from Czechoslovakia who saved thousands of Jews from almost certain death at the hands of the Nazis.

3. This unlikely hero was: Oskar Schindler, drinker, gambler, womanizer, and black market profiteer.

4. The movie features an extraordinary cast Liam Neeson as Schindler, Ben Kingsley as Itzhak Stern, Schindler's Jewish business adviser and friend, and Ralph Fiennes as Amon Goeth, the brutal and corrupt commander of a slave labor camp in Nazi-occupied Poland.

5. This Oscar winning-movie was later shown—on television—without commercial interruption; only a few minutes of the original three and a half hour film were cut by Spielberg himself for the Ford sponsored broadcast on NBC.

6. The TV broadcast of *Schindler's List* was viewed by sixty five million people; more than twice the number who saw the big screen version in movie theaters.

7. Many viewers probably did not realize that the movie was based on a 1982 book (originally published in England as: *Schindler's Ark*) by the Australian writer Thomas Keneally.

8. Keneally first heard about Oskar Schindler when he was shopping at a Beverly Hills luggage store owned by one of the Jews whom Schindler saved: Leopold Pfefferberg.

9. Keneally's book won England's 1982 Booker Prize for Fiction the nation's best known literary award.

10. Keneally's victory generated a huge controversy in England; because in the preface the author insists that his book is not a work of fiction he describes it instead as a "documentary novel" that tells a true story.

Chapter 38: Capitalization

38-1: Capitalizing (1)

Edit the following sentences by capitalizing as needed.

EXAMPLE

    I   N   Y   C
In new york city you can probably find people from almost every
                     E   *M*   *E*   *A*   *A*
region of the world—europe, the middle east, asia, africa—and plenty
         N   Y
of native new yorkers, too.

1. according to an article in the *new york times magazine,* more and more americans are rejecting their parents' religion.

2. in an article entitled "choosing my religion," stephen j. dubner analyzes a trend that affects him on a personal level.

3. dubner, who is an editor at the magazine, grew up in a large catholic family.

4. his parents, however, both grew up jewish and converted to catholicism when they were in their twenties.

5. his mother, florence greenglass, and his father, solomon dubner, were both born in brooklyn, the children of russian and polish immigrants.

6. when florence greenglass was baptized a roman catholic, she chose "veronica" as her baptismal name; solomon chose the name "paul."

7. they were married on march 2, 1946, at st. brigid's catholic church in brooklyn; none of their families attended the wedding.

8. stephen dubner, the youngest of eight children, grew up on a farm in upstate new york, near the town of duanesburg.

9. his family was devoutly catholic, but by the time dubner left home for college, he had become uncomfortable with his religion.

10. under the guidance of his friend ivan, dubner began exploring judaism and learning hebrew while he was in graduate school.

38-2: Capitalizing (2)

Edit the following sentences by correcting errors in capitalization.

EXAMPLE

I appreciate the architecture of all different ~~R~~eligions' places of
worship, such as Jewish ~~T~~emples, ~~c~~hristian churches, and Islamic
mosques.

1. According to Dean Hoge, a Sociology Professor at Catholic university
   in washington, D.C., switching religions is more common in America
   today than it has ever been in history.

2. In their book *One nation under God,* Barry a. kosmin and seymour p.
   Lachman estimate that 30 percent of Americans switch religions or
   denominations during their lifetimes.

3. Most of these people switch from one Protestant Denomination to
   another, but some changes are more dramatic.

4. Kosmin and lachman, who surveyed 113,000 people for their book,
   concluded that the most common reason for switching religions is
   intermarriage—marrying someone of a different Faith.

5. In his *New york times magazine* article "Choosing my Religion," Stephen
   J. dubner explores his own switch from catholicism to judaism, but he
   also spotlights several other young americans who have changed religions.

6. Daniel Dunn grew up a congregationalist but became a catholic after
   he almost died in a serious water-skiing accident.

7. Judith Anderson grew up in a jewish family in Teaneck, New jersey,
   but she is now a buddhist.

8. Like many jews who practice buddhism, Anderson has not renounced
   her Judaism; instead, she feels that she has added another Spiritual
   layer to her life.

9. Fatima shama is the Daughter of a devoutly Catholic brazilian
   mother and a muslim palestinian father who isn't very religious.

10. She grew up Catholic in the bronx but began practicing a liberal
    form of islam during College.

Answer Keys

Answer Key—Supplemental Exercises for Chapter 18 ("Writing the Research Essay")

Answers to Exercises 18-1 through 18-5 will vary. Possible answers are given below.

Answers to 18-1

Possible answers:

SUMMARY

Recent scientific findings suggest that the human brain is preprogrammed for music (Begley 51).

PARAPHRASE

Humans can store a large number of songs in their memory, compelling evidence that our minds are preprogrammed for music. By contrast, people rarely remember more than a few sentences of written material (Begley 51).

DIRECT QUOTE

As Begley states, "several lines of evidence suggest that the human brain is wired for music" (51).

Answers to 18-2

Possible answers:

SUMMARY

Feng shui, an ancient Chinese method of designing and organizing spaces to maximize energy and bring wealth, has become a trend in modern interior design (Singh 53).

PARAPHRASE

Feng shui relies on *qi,* energy that can be affected by a space's character—its shape and dimensions. A building with good feng shui, which allows *qi* to move freely throughout a space, rewards its owner with worldly success (Singh 53).

DIRECT QUOTE

As Singh states, "A building that allows *qi* to flow freely is said to have good feng shui" (53).

Answers to 18-3

Possible answers:

SUMMARY

Snitching helps the government and law enforcement relieve an over-populated criminal system, but using snitching as a crime fighting tool is a method charged with complexities (Natapoff 705).

PARAPHRASE

Snitching allows criminals to control police activity and dangerous criminals can often evade consequences by snitching on other criminals. Yet for law enforcement, snitching has become an easy and often overused tool for an overpopulated system without the means to prosecute and house so many criminals (Natapoff 705).

DIRECT QUOTE

Natapoff points to the consequences of snitching, stating, "often the snitches are more dangerous than the targets" (705).

Answers to 18-4

Possible answers:

SUMMARY

Stereotypes and clichés are substitutes for thinking and getting to know people as individuals rather than as members of a group (Ericsson 664).

PARAPHRASE

In today's world, the need to process a great deal of information quickly leads to the use of stereotypes (Ericsson 664).

DIRECT QUOTE

According to Ericsson, a stereotype "explains a situation with just enough truth to seem unquestionable" (664).

Answers to 18-5

Possible answers:

SUMMARY

People have long wondered whether money can buy happiness. Some new research suggests that it can—if you spend your money on other people, not yourself (Tierney 692).

PARAPHRASE

In a large national survey of 600 people, researchers found that people became happier when they spent their money on others rather than on themselves (Tierney 692).

DIRECT QUOTE

As Tierney notes, researchers "found that spending more on gifts and charity correlated with greater happiness, whereas spending more money on oneself did not" (692).

Answer Key—Supplemental Exercises for Editing Chapters (*Chapters 19–38*)

Answers to 19-1

1. adjective.	6. conjunction.
2. verb.	7. noun.
3. adverb.	8. pronoun.
4. pronoun.	9. verb.
5. preposition.	10. adverb.

Answers to 19-2

1. *The Perfect Storm.*	6. *Andrea Gail.*
2. it.	7. boat.
3. book.	8. messages.
4. one.	9. crew.
5. "perfect storm."	10. *Andrea Gail.*

Answers to 19-3

1. helping + main verb.
2. linking verb.
3. action verb.
4. action verb.
5. action verb.
6. action verb.
7. action verb.
8. helping + main verb.
9. linking verb.
10. helping + main verb.

Answers to 19-4

1. I.	6. C.
2. C.	7. I.
3. C.	8. C.
4. I.	9. I.
5. C.	10. C.

Answers to 20-1

1. In 1976, twenty-one-year-old Steven Jobs cofounded Apple Computer, Inc., in his family's garage.
2. In 1984, the team Jobs led created the Apple Macintosh computer, with its user-friendly "point and click" operating system.
3. Yet one year later, Jobs was forced out of his own company by the board of directors.
4. Over the next few years, the Mac revolutionized the computer world.
5. Apple's rival, the Microsoft Corporation, modeled its Windows operating system on the Mac.
6. After leaving Apple, Jobs started a computer company called NeXT that developed a cutting-edge new operating system.
7. A British computer programmer created the World Wide Web on the NeXT system.
8. In 1986, Jobs bought Pixar, a small computer animation studio, from the film director George Lucas.
9. Pixar created the animation for the 1995 hit movie *Toy Story*.
10. In late 1996, Jobs stunned the computer industry by selling NeXT and its operating system to his old company, Apple.

Answers to 20-2

1. The zoologist Frans de Waal has spent the past twenty-five years studying how apes and monkeys behave in captivity.
2. He is a professor of primate behavior at Emory University in Atlanta, where he is also a researcher at the Yerkes Regional Primate Research Center.
3. While many scientists have emphasized the role of aggression in animal behavior, de Waal stresses the importance of animal kindness and caring.
4. Although animals clearly have rivals, he believes they also have friends.
5. Each group of chimpanzees has a leader, though de Waal thinks it is the one who makes the best friendships and alliances rather than the one who is the most aggressive.
6. His research on animal relationships has shown that capuchin monkeys will

repeatedly find ways to share food when they are separated from each other by a mesh screen.

7. This sharing is a deliberate choice because the monkeys share only with monkeys they like.

8. De Waal believes that the stereotype of the killer-ape is harmful, since it suggests that human nature is essentially violent and cruel.

9. He argues that morality is an outgrowth of our natural instincts, which are automatic responses that all people have.

10. If we want to understand what makes us naturally aggressive, we also have to understand what makes us naturally caring.

Answers to 20-3

1. Sharon Bearor was sitting in a doctor's office at Massachusetts General Hospital listening to Dr. Allen Lapey explain her son's options.

2. Suffering from cystic fibrosis, nineteen-year-old Spencer Bean needed two new lungs.

3. However, the long waiting list for an organ donation meant Spencer might die waiting for a pair of lungs to become available.

4. Reaching the top of the list, he might also be too sick to go through with the transplant operation.

5. Explaining that there was another option, Dr. Lapey told Spencer and Sharon about an experimental new medical procedure.

6. Doctors could replace a patient's diseased lungs using healthy lung tissue from two living relatives.

7. Realizing that Spencer might die without their help, Sharon and her sister Jean decided to donate part of their lungs.

8. Some people are opposed to living-donor transplants, believing it's unethical to risk harming a healthy person.

9. They also argue that some people might feel pressured to donate organs, fearing their family's anger if they say no.

10. Ignoring complicated questions of medical ethics, Sharon and Jean simply did what they thought was right.

Answers to 20-4

POSSIBLE REVISIONS

1. Some parents are so fed up with television programming that they want one thing from their families: They long for them to kick the TV habit.

2. Producer Linda Ellerbee once threw her TV set out of a second-story window to get her children's attention when they were watching television.

3. To appease her guilt later in the day, she went out to retrieve the television from her yard. To her amazement, when she plugged it in, it still worked.

4. To study the problem, the Annenberg Public Policy Center has conducted three studies.

5. Parents can use ratings attached to many programs and V-chip technology to block certain shows they do not want their children to see.

6. Few parents use either method, and most reported they felt powerless to control their children's viewing habits.

7. According to one researcher, parents have an important role to play. They should serve as examples of how much television is acceptable.

8. To give a child his or her own television solves many arguments about what to watch, but researchers suggest that this solution means that parents do not know how much television their child is watching.

9. One mother decided to unplug her television one night a week. She intended to show her family that they could survive without television.

10. She reported that everyone struggled, including herself. To keep everyone occupied and busy through the first few weeks, she used all her creative abilities planning activities.

Answers to 20-5

1. Arthur Caplan is a professor of bioethics, the study of ethical issues relating to medicine, health care, and science.
2. He analyzes complex moral questions, such as whether society should allow doctor-assisted suicide.
3. Bioethical issues are often featured on TV hospital shows like *Grey's Anatomy* and the former hit *Chicago Hope*.
4. Caplan thinks these shows do an okay job of exploring certain bioethical issues, including the question of whether to give an alcoholic a liver transplant.
5. However, he feels they don't pay enough attention to other kinds of issues, particularly those relating to money.
6. An episode of *Chicago Hope* was based on one of Caplan's actual cases, a heart transplant in which the doctors didn't know if they had to tell the patient they had dropped the heart on the floor.
7. Caplan believes that it is sometimes ethical to lie, especially if a life is at stake.
8. He thinks a doctor should lie to help a patient who is being pressured by family members, as in the case of someone who is refusing a blood transfusion for religious reasons.
9. A doctor should also give a phony medical excuse to a family member who doesn't want to donate a live organ, such as a kidney or lung.
10. Here the moral issue is free choice, not saving a life, as in the example of the blood transfusion.

Answers to 20-6

1. Have you ever wondered how a microwave oven cooks food without heating the plate?
2. A microwave is an electromagnetic wave ranging in frequency from around 1,000 to 300,000 megahertz (MHz).
3. An electromagnetic wave is a vibration resulting from the motion of positive and negative electrical charges.
4. There are many different kinds of electromagnetic waves, such as electric waves, radio waves, infrared radiation, visible light, ultraviolet radiation, X-rays, and gamma rays.
5. Microwaves cook food quickly by making the water molecules in the food vibrate at a rate of 2,450 million times per second.
6. This vibration absorbs energy from the surrounding electromagnetic field, causing the food to heat up.
7. The plate and utensils don't get hot because their materials don't absorb energy from the magnetic field.
8. Since all the energy is absorbed by the food, microwave cooking is faster than regular cooking.
9. Many different materials are safe to use in a microwave oven, like china, glass, plastic, and paper.
10. But you should not use items made out of metal or wood when you microwave, to prevent damage to those items.

Answers to 20-7

1. Velcro was invented by the Swiss engineer George de Mestral after he took a walk in the woods with his dog.
2. Arriving back home, he noticed that his socks and his dog were covered with burrs.
3. De Mestral wanted to find out why burrs stick so well to certain materials, such as wool and fur.
4. Looking at his socks under the microscope, he discovered that tiny hooks on the ends of the burrs were caught in the wool's loops.
5. De Mestral figured out a way to copy this natural system of hooks and loops.
6. He wove nylon thread into a fabric containing densely packed little loops.
7. He cut the loops on some of the fabric to make half of each loop a hook.
8. De Mestral called this fabric Velcro, a contraction of the French words *velours* (velvet) and *crochet* (hook).

9. Although Velcro can be peeled apart quite easily, it has extremely high resistance to sideways forces.

10. Velcro has been used to prevent equipment, and even astronauts, from floating around in the space shuttle.

Answers to 21-1

1. Lead pencils don't really contain any lead. They're made out of graphite. **RO**

2. Lead hasn't been used in pencils since the sixteenth century. It's a good thing because lead is poisonous. **CS**

3. The ancient Egyptians, Greeks, and Romans used small lead discs to make lines on sheets of papyrus. Then they wrote on the papyrus with ink and a brush. **CS**

4. During the fourteenth century European artists made drawings using rods of lead, zinc, or silver. The technique was called silverpoint. **RO**

5. Wood-encased writing rods were used during the fifteenth century. They were the earliest pencils. **CS**

6. The modern pencil was developed in 1564.That's when graphite was discovered in Borrowdale, England. **RO**

7. Graphite is a form of carbon. It's greasy and soft with a metallic luster. **RO**

8. Pencil "lead" is made by mixing graphite with clay and water. Then the mixture is fed into a thin cylinder to create sticks. **CS**

9. More graphite in the mixture makes the pencil softer and blacker. More clay makes it harder and paler. **CS**

10. The sticks are cut into pencil-sized lengths. Then they are fired in a kiln at a temperature of about 2200°F (1200°C). **RO**

Answers to 21-2

1. For years, child development specialists have recommended that parents pick up crying babies as soon as possible; even two minutes of crying can be considered excessive.

2. These experts say that parents should be especially attentive to children under six months of age; tiny babies need reassurance that someone will meet their needs.

3. Letting babies cry too long can raise their blood pressure and levels of stress hormones; it can even interfere with their emotional development, some specialists say.

4. However, some child development experts think that letting a baby cry for a few minutes is not harmful; in fact, it can help parents get their children on a consistent sleeping and feeding schedule.

5. For instance, if a baby cries when it's not her usual feeding time, the parents might let her cry and feed her at her regular time; this approach is sometimes known as "controlled crying."

6. In the future, say advocates of this approach, the baby will be more likely to keep to a regular feeding schedule and less likely to cry; others disagree.

7. Opponents of controlled crying say it doesn't guarantee that babies will behave better; it might even cause them to feel unloved.

8. These experts often hear criticism that children who are picked up as soon as they cry will become spoiled; their response is essentially "Nonsense."

9. These experts say that responsive parents prove to babies that they can count on their mother and father; this trust is crucial to children's well-being and development.

10. Pediatrician William Sears says that parents should put themselves in the crying child's position and ask what they would want the mother or father to do; he is sure the answer would be to pick up the child.

Answers to 21-3

POSSIBLE REVISIONS

1. Don't believe everything you learn about animals from Hollywood movies, or you might come away misinformed.

2. For example, the 1994 movie *Andre the Seal* is based on a true story about a New England harbor seal, but the title character is played by a California sea lion.

3. The real Andre was five feet long and weighed 250 pounds, but the sea lion actor is twice as big.
4. The decision to cast a solid-brown sea lion as a spotted gray seal may seem ridiculous, yet the filmmakers had their reasons.
5. Unlike sea lions, harbor seals don't have huge front flippers, so they can't scoot around very well.
6. Seals can't do cute tricks on land with human actors, for they spend most of their time in the water.
7. In the 1995 movie *Outbreak,* a monkey brings a deadly African virus to America, yet the monkey is actually played by a South American capuchin monkey.
8. That's because capuchins are more readily available than African monkeys, and they are easier to train.
9. You might assume that the 1988 movie *Gorillas in the Mist* portrays animals accurately, for it was filmed on location in Africa among a band of mountain gorillas.
10. However, wild mother gorillas won't let humans touch their young, so in one scene a baby gorilla is really a chimpanzee in a gorilla suit.

Answers to 21-4

POSSIBLE REVISIONS

1. Kristin Hersh is a working mother, although she has a rather unusual job.
2. While Hersh is raising her children, she has both a solo career and is the lead singer and guitarist for the band Throwing Muses.
3. Her husband, Billy O'Connell, understands her unconventional career choice because he's the band's manager.
4. Hersh has combined rock and roll and motherhood since she had her first child at the age of nineteen.
5. Her oldest son Dylan now lives with his father most of the year, though he spends vacations with his mother and stepfather.

6. When Hersh goes on tour, sons Ryder, Wyatt, and Bodhi will be traveling with their parents.
7. Hersh thinks the rock world is beginning to change, although it is still uncommon to see children on the tour bus.
8. As more women performers are becoming mothers, more kids are being nursed backstage and rocked to sleep in dressing rooms.
9. Hersh and O'Connell waited to let their older sons watch their mom perform, since most shows are so loud and smoky.
10. The boys watched a smoke-free acoustic show when Hersh was pregnant.

Answers to 21-5

POSSIBLE REVISIONS

1. Nathan Kane began inventing when he was eighteen years old.
2. Kane wanted to create a dust-free environment in their Texas home because his father suffered from allergies.
3. Ten years later, he won a $30,000 prize for young inventors. The award was presented by the Massachusetts Institute of Technology.
4. Kane was a graduate student at MIT; he was studying mechanical engineering.
5. He thought of the idea for one of his inventions while he was refinishing the floors in his parents' house.
6. It was very hot, so he was uncomfortable wearing a regular filter mask.
7. Kane invented a mask that supplies fresh air through a flexible hose. The hose is really a lightweight bellows.
8. Though bellows have been used for thousands of years, Kane came up with a better design.
9. He and a friend invented a TV remote control that's hard to lose and easy to pass around; it's built inside a foam rubber football.
10. Kane recently served as an adviser to a group of middle-school students as they designed solar-powered model cars.

Answers to 21-6

POSSIBLE REVISIONS

1. Tom Scott and Tom First began selling juice in 1989 when they were twenty-four years old.
2. They had been friends since freshman year in college, and they moved to the island of Nantucket soon after graduation.
3. Their business began as a floating juice bar in Nantucket Harbor; they sold glasses of homemade peach juice off the deck of their boat.
4. Soon Scott and First began bottling their juice by hand. The following summer it was being professionally packaged in New York and distributed throughout Nantucket, Martha's Vineyard, and Cape Cod.
5. Their juice is called Nantucket Nectars, but the name of their company is Nantucket Allserve.
6. Sales and production increased dramatically over the next few years, yet the company was still struggling to survive.
7. In 1993, an investor bought half the company for $500,000; that money allowed Scott and First to expand their markets and product line.
8. Although Scott and First have no formal business training, Nantucket Allserve was one of the nation's fastest-growing private companies.
9. Their juice is sold in more than forty states, and their company is worth $30 million.
10. Although the company is now owned by the Dr. Pepper Snapple Group, Scott and First still voice the radio ads.

Answers to 22-1

1. Subject: region; verb: was.
2. Subject: it; verb: was.
3. Subject: blizzard; verb: has.
4. Subject: I; verb: don't.
5. Subject: schools; verb: are.
6. Subject: I; verb: have.
7. Subject: neighbors; verb: are.
8. Subject: family; verb: has.
9. Subject: people; verb: have.
10. Subject: I; verb: am.

Answers to 22-2

1. Prepositional phrase: in hiring practices; verb: is.
2. Prepositional phrase: of job applicants; verb: is.
3. Prepositional phrase: of comparison between hiring outcomes; verb: is.
4. Prepositional phrase: of orchestra hiring practices; verb: finds.
5. Prepositional phrase: throughout the country; verb: use.
6. Prepositional phrase: for a position with the orchestra; verb: perform.
7. Prepositional phrase: at major orchestras; verb: improves.
8. Prepositional phrase: of female musicians in the top five American orchestras; verb: is.
9. Prepositional phrase: of orchestras; verb: reports.
10. Prepositional phrase: to blind auditions; verb: explains.

Answers to 22-3

1. Dependent clause: that Indian women wear on their foreheads; verb: indicates.
2. Dependent clause: which is known as a *bindi* or *pottu;* verb: represents.
3. Dependent clause: which was originally a simple red or maroon powdered circle; verb: has evolved.
4. Dependent clause: who wore *bindis;* verb: were. **OK**
5. Dependent clause: that Hindu women have worn for centuries; verb: is.
6. Dependent clause: whose *bindi* first attracted attention among trendy, pierced people; verb: was.
7. Dependent clause: who is the lead singer of the band No Doubt; verb: wore.
8. Dependent clause: whom many people have compared to Madonna; verb: liked.
9. Dependent clause: that is a favorite among southern Indian women; verb: looked.

10. Dependent clause: which was once a meaningful religious symbol; verb: was.
 OK

Answers to 22-4

1. Compound subject: The orangutan, gorilla, chimpanzee, and bonobo; verb: are.
2. Compound subject: the chimp and the gorilla; verb: look.
3. Compound subject: the chimpanzee and the bonobo; verb: share.
4. Compound subject: Chimpanzees and humans; verb: are.
5. Compound subject: Murder, rape, torture, gang warfare, and territorial raiding; verb: occur.
6. Compound subject: The chimpanzee and the bonobo; verb: are; compound subject: chimps and humans; verb: are.
7. Compound subject: The male and female bonobo; verb: have.
8. Compound subject: a mother bonobo or her son; verb: is.
9. Compound subject: The status or power; verb: depends.
10. Compound subject: the chimpanzee or the bonobo; verb: is.

Answers to 22-5

1. Subject: Everyone; prepositional phrase: in my college writing class; verb: speaks.
2. Subject: few; prepositional phrase: of the students; verb: are.
3. Subject: Many; prepositional phrase: of the students; verb: are.
4. Subject: Several; prepositional phrase: of the best students in the class; verb: are.
5. Subject: One; prepositional phrase: of my closest friends in the class; verb: comes.
6. Subject: Both; prepositional phrase: of us; verb: live.
7. Subject: No one; prepositional phrase: in my class; verb: speaks.
8. Subject: Each; prepositional phrase: of us; verb: studies.
9. Subject: none; prepositional phrase: of my hard work; verb: seems.

10. Subject: Neither; prepositional phrase: of my parents; verb: speaks.

Answers to 22-6

1. are.	6. are.
2. **OK.**	7. Are.
3. Have.	8. Do.
4. are.	9. are.
5. **OK.**	10. **OK.**

Answers to 22-7

1. Subject: Commuting; verb: is.
2. Subject: Many; verb: have.
3. Subject: Travel; verb: has become.
4. Subject: commuting; verb: remains.
5. Subject: Businesses; verb: continue.
6. Subject: Telecommuters; verb: work.
7. Subject: Companies; verb: report.
8. Subject: Collaboration and feedback; verb: happen.
9. Subject: Community colleges and universities; verb: are.
10. Subject: you; verb: have.

Answers to 23-1

1. explain.	6. feel.
2. stop.	7. loves.
3. use.	8. prefer.
4. offers.	9. think.
5. take.	10. keeps.

Answers to 23-2

1. specialized.	6. helped.
2. rescued.	7. chased.
3. pulled.	8. scared.
4. resulted.	9. retrieved.
5. used.	10. earned.

Answers to 23-3

1. applied.	6. helps.
2. hope.	7. want.
3. searched.	8. increased.
4. checked.	9. need.
5. showed.	10. cost.

Answers to 23-4

1. am.
2. have.
3. am.
4. have.
5. am.
6. am.
7. have.
8. has.
9. is.
10. are.

Answers to 23-5

1. grew.
2. began.
3. took.
4. was.
5. hit.
6. brought.
7. taught.
8. quit.
9. knew.
10. said.

Answers to 23-6

1. ate.
2. made.
3. thought.
4. had.
5. brought.
6. said.
7. knew.
8. lost.
9. told.
10. quit.

Answers to 23-7

1. tried.
2. worked.
3. waited.
4. helped.
5. parked.
6. prepared.
7. allowed.
8. realized.
9. registered.
10. expanded.

Answers to 23-8

1. begun.
2. become.
3. caught.
4. created.
5. found.
6. done.
7. picked.
8. shown.
9. fallen.
10. made.

Answers to 23-9

1. was.
2. became.
3. have stayed.
4. began.
5. has gotten.
6. lost.
7. has applied.
8. decided.
9. have attended.
10. felt.

Answers to 23-10

1. have raised.
2. has investigated.
3. has stated.
4. has shown.
5. has announced.
6. have argued.
7. have created.
8. have helped.
9. have prevented.
10. have written.

Answers to 23-11

1. became.
2. had thought.
3. had seen.
4. had been.
5. had tried.
6. found.
7. had worked.
8. stopped.
9. had known.
10. had kept.

Answers to 23-12

1. had held.
2. had dropped out.
3. had been.
4. had worked.
5. had figured out.
6. had realized.
7. had managed.
8. had received.
9. had learned.
10. had not tried.

Answers to 23-13

1. **A;** subject: I; verb: completed.
2. **P;** subject: a lot; verb: was taught.
3. **P;** subject: it; verb: was suggested.
4. **P;** subject: letters; verb: were sent.
5. **A;** subject: I; verb: mentioned.
6. **P;** subject: letters; verb: were sent.
7. **A;** subject: companies; verb: called.
8. **P;** subject: job; verb: was offered.
9. **A;** subject: I; verb: accepted.
10. **P;** subject: workers; verb: are needed.

Answers to 23-14

POSSIBLE REVISIONS

1. Several student organizations that are working together to oppose the increase in parking rates took a poll.
2. Ninety percent of the students who drive to school voted that the increase is too high.
3. "The rates were already high, and now they have more than doubled," one student remarked.
4. The students recognize that the state has given the college less money this year.
5. The college should not force students who drive to school to make up the entire amount of money cut by the state.
6. In most cases, only students who don't live near public transportation resort to driving to school.
7. Some of these students will find paying the increased rate impossible.

8. Students who come to class after work don't have enough time to drive to a subway station and then take the subway to school.
9. The expensive parking rates may discourage some people from applying to the college at all.
10. The college should raise funds in a way that is fair to all students.

Answers to 23-15

POSSIBLE REVISIONS

1. No drinks or food should be brought into the library.
2. A drink was brought into the library the other day.
3. A drink was spilled on a book.
4. The ruined book was found on Tuesday.
5. My friend and I were reported to the librarians.
6. Our library cards were revoked the following day.
7. We were denied the chance to plead our case.
8. The dean was told by a professor how unfair our case was.
9. We were not seen spilling the drink on the book.
10. It is stated by the law that rights and privileges cannot be revoked based on circumstantial evidence.

Answers to 23-16

1. is.
2. won.
3. is; is.
4. told; had; had.
5. gave; refused.
6. endured.
7. survived; improved.
8. is.
9. has; has.
10. wear; sells.

Answers to 23-17

1. read.
2. found.
3. ask.
4. has raised.
5. gave.
6. listen.
7. post.
8. are.
9. erase.
10. are.

Answers to 23-18

1. is.
2. has grown.
3. have seen.
4. lies.
5. painted.
6. has decayed.
7. began; finished.
8. used; gave; made.
9. have been.
10. began; has reversed.

Answers to 24-1

1. all.
2. they.
3. they.
4. she; she.
5. her; they.
6. their.
7. their.
8. their.
9. they.
10. they.

Answers to 24-2

1. it.
2. his or her.
3. she.
4. they.
5. its.
6. itself.
7. their jobs.
8. it.
9. it.
10. it.

Answers to 24-3

1. he or she.
2. their.
3. his or her.
4. his or her.
5. his or her.
6. their.
7. his or her.
8. they.
9. we.
10. their.

Answers to 24-4

1. its.
2. it.
3. its.
4. its.
5. it.
6. its.
7. it.
8. itself.
9. its.
10. it.

Answers to 24-5

POSSIBLE REVISIONS

1. Yesterday, I got a letter from my doctor informing me that she and her partner were no longer accepting my insurance plan.
2. Dr. Reuter and her partner, Dr. Spingarn, have decided not to go along with the insurance company's new way of paying doctors.

3. According to the letter, my insurance company is now forcing doctors to accept capitation, a payment method that my doctor describes as "unethical."

4. With this payment method, every month the doctor gets a fixed fee for each patient, no matter how much treatment the doctor provides.

5. In other words, doctors are paid the same amount whether a patient needs six office visits a month or none.

6. With the traditional fee-for-service method of reimbursement, insurance companies pay doctors every time they treat a patient.

7. My doctor and her partner believe that capitation is bad because it rewards doctors for providing less medical care and penalizes them for providing more.

8. They think it creates a conflict of interest between doctors and patients because doctors have a financial incentive to withhold treatment.

9. Dr. Reuter and Dr. Spingarn decided that they could not accept the capitation plan even if rejecting it meant losing patients who could not switch to a different insurance company.

10. When I called my insurance company to complain about capitation, the customer service representative told me that the company was simply trying to keep my premiums down by controlling medical costs.

Answers to 24-6

1. Last March, my friend Elena and I both had babies, five days apart.

2. Everyone in the neighborhood gave Elena and me a double baby shower, with matching outfits for our two kids.

3. **OK.**

4. Unfortunately, now that I'm in school and Elena is back at her job, she and I don't see each other as much as we used to.

5. Sometimes, Max and I run into her and Lucy at the playground or the library.

6. When we saw Lucy and her the other day, Elena was complaining that she and her husband, Danny, never spend any time together anymore.

7. They're always so tired and stressed out from working and taking care of Lucy that when she and Danny do see each other, they just end up arguing.

8. **OK.**

9. The other day she said, "If things don't get better between him and me, Danny and I are going to end up getting a divorce."

10. I told her that David and I had struggled with the same issue and that I thought they would work things out if they could just spend more time together.

Answers to 24-7

1. My older sister, Nadine, always seems to get her schoolwork done faster than I.

2. Nadine does better on tests, but I write better papers than she.

3. As a result, she usually gets about the same grades as I.

4. **OK.**

5. The whole time we were growing up, teachers always seemed to like her better than me.

6. **OK.**

7. Nadine is eighteen months older than I, but people always ask us if we're twins.

8. **OK.**

9. I guess deep down inside I'm worried that people will respect her more than me or think she's smarter than I.

10. I don't understand why I'm so competitive with Nadine, since I don't know any sisters who are closer friends than we.

Answers to 24-8

1. who.	6. who.
2. whom.	7. whoever.
3. who.	8. who.
4. who.	9. whom.
5. whom.	10. whom.

Answers for 24-9

1. Many students and professionals do not realize that writing can provide **them** with a means of achieving goals.
2. They need to understand that writing down **their** goals is better than just thinking about them.
3. When someone writes down a goal, one part of his or her brain starts collecting pertinent information and sends it to the conscious part of **his or her** mind.
4. Thus, the person starts to recognize opportunities **he or she** never would have noticed otherwise.
5. When **they** put **their** goals on paper, people need to include both short- and long-term goals.
6. People who try this technique should not worry about **their** spelling or edit **their** ideas.
7. If students have trouble writing goals, **they** might want to write down on another sheet what is keeping **them** from reaching **their** goals.
8. By being specific rather than vague, people can more easily decide how to meet **their** goals.
9. To help focus on the outcome, a person may want to include smaller goals that are steps to the final goal.
10. People who follow this technique have learned that the fears that could keep them from succeeding become more manageable if **they** write those fears down.

Answers to 25-1

1. mischievous **character.**
2. greedy **troublemaker.**
3. **is** usually.
4. foolish **pranks.**
5. secretly **admire.**
6. powerful **opponents.**
7. unexpected **ways.**
8. popular **tricksters.**
9. sensible **friend.**
10. Uncontrollably **curious.**

Answers to 25-2

1. most famous.
2. more famous.
3. most important.
4. stronger; more clever.
5. easier.
6. harder.
7. smaller; bigger.
8. larger.
9. higher.
10. more difficult.

Answers to 25-3

1. good.	6. good.
2. worse.	7. badly.
3. badly.	8. better.
4. better.	9. worst.
5. best.	10. bad.

Answers to 26-1

POSSIBLE REVISIONS

1. We have been building an addition onto our house for the past four months.
2. The addition will be a sunroom that will be lit almost entirely with natural light.
3. I have wanted a room surrounded by windows, like this one, for a long time.
4. Using material recycled from the garage we are tearing down, we are building the addition fairly inexpensively.
5. The cedar planks that once served as garage siding will look charmingly rustic in our new room.
6. We have also taken skylights that were once over the bedroom closet and moved them to the sunroom's roof.
7. We found an old glass door in our attic that we can use for the doorway between the sunroom and the backyard.
8. To do the floor ourselves, though, seemed like an impossible job, so without hesitation we hired a contractor.
9. When we are nearly done with sheet-rocking the walls, he can come in and begin laying out the frame for the floor.

10. I can't wait until we can begin eating in our soon-to-be-finished new room.

Answers to 26-2

POSSIBLE REVISIONS

1. Armed and well trained, five elite Coast Guard divers raided a yacht yesterday where four people were being held hostage.
2. The hostages, a woman and her three children, were unharmed.
3. Scared of the hijacker, the captain began to sail the yacht off its original course.
4. Wanting to go to Greece, the hijacker demanded that the yacht begin heading east.
5. Bravely, the captain sent a secret message to the Coast Guard and foiled the hijacker's plans.
6. Picking up the signal, the Coast Guard acted swiftly and effectively.
7. Distracted by three Coast Guard boats surrounding the front of the yacht, the hijacker did not even notice the divers climbing aboard the back of the yacht.
8. Motioning to the hostages to keep quiet, the divers crept up front to start the ambush while the boats outside kept the hijacker distracted.
9. Unwilling to give in, the hijacker began firing.
10. Trained to fire back when necessary, the Coast Guard divers shot the hijacker.

Answers to 26-3

POSSIBLE REVISIONS

1. Getting to work from my house by subway takes only about twenty minutes.
2. While riding the subway, you can pass the time quickly if you have something to read.
3. I used to take the bus to work instead of the subway, but the bus is slower.
4. The bus takes nearly twice as long as the subway because of all the traffic.
5. Also, the bus stops at almost every corner.
6. Having taken the bus for years, I had never considered trying the subway.

7. Though rather noisy, the subway is better because I can read without getting a headache.
8. Riding the subway for a year, I haven't gotten a headache even once.
9. Reading on the bus, I found that my head would start throbbing after five minutes.
10. Unable to read, I could only stare out the window.

Answers to 26-4

POSSIBLE REVISIONS

1. While we were painting our living room, our black cat pushed open the door and rubbed up against the wet molding.
2. Looking like a skunk, Lucy was hiding under the bed when we found her.
3. We had painted the molding with oil-based paint, which was now on her fur.
4. After considering our other options, we decided to clean her fur with paint thinner.
5. Now covered with paint thinner, Lucy needed to be washed and rinsed with soap and water.
6. Cleaning our brushes in the basement an hour later, we realized that we had made a terrible mistake.
7. We found Lucy, usually so gentle and affectionate, hissing and arching her back at us.
8. We rushed her to the emergency animal hospital, where the vet told us that you should never use paint thinner on an animal.
9. During our conversation with the vet, we learned that we should have used just soap and water or a lanolin hand cleaner.
10. Grateful that she was okay, we took Lucy home after she had been sedated and thoroughly bathed.

Answers to 27-1

1. and.	6. nor.
2. but.	7. for.
3. so.	8. but.
4. and.	9. or.
5. for.	10. and.

Answers to 27-2

1. Sports that have historically been considered off-limits to women are changing; women are beginning to participate in professional athletics in areas where they have never competed before.
2. One example is weightlifting; at seventeen, Cheryl Haworth became the most well-known female weightlifter.
3. Haworth is five feet nine inches tall and weighs 300 pounds; she has the ideal build for a weightlifter.
4. She can lift over 300 pounds; this power made her the medal favorite at the 2000 Olympics.
5. She lifts as much as 25 tons in the course of her daily workout; every day she lifts the equivalent of five elephants or one F-15 fighter jet.
6. Haworth is also something of a practical jokester; she has been known to lift her friend's car and move it to a different location.
7. Haworth's thighs measure 32 inches in circumference; she can bench press 500 pounds.
8. She began lifting weights when she was twelve years old and already weighed 240 pounds; she could lift over 110 pounds.
9. She also has the speed and flexibility needed by a great weightlifter; she can run a 40-yard dash in five seconds.
10. Haworth called for significant changes in women's sports; the inclusion of female weightlifting for the first time in the 2000 Olympics was proof of these changes.

Answers to 27-3
POSSIBLE REVISIONS

1. My friend Simone became pregnant when she was a junior in college; as a result, she could not go back to finish her senior year.
2. She could not afford child care; therefore, she had to stay home after Danny, her son, was born.
3. Danny is five now and is beginning kindergarten next month; as a result, Simone will have five hours free every day.

4. Simone has signed up for two morning classes in nursing at her community college; in addition, she has applied for a part-time job at a nursing home.
5. It won't be easy fitting work and classes into her busy parenting schedule; however, Simone feels that Danny will be better off when they are financially secure.
6. There are things she would like to buy for Danny that she cannot afford; also, Simone wants to show Danny that she can beat the odds.
7. Simone would like to eventually be a nurse; in fact, through caring for Danny, she's already had some practice as one.
8. The three-year course to become a certified nurse is too much for Simone; instead, she could take fewer classes and become a nurse practitioner.
9. Either way, she would be working with patients; in addition, she would be making good use of her naturally caring personality.
10. Simone says she is glad that things turned out as they did with her schooling because she feels more dedicated now than she did five years ago; besides, she has a wonderful son in her life.

Answers to 27-4
POSSIBLE REVISIONS

1. My car started making a funny noise, so I took it to the repair shop down the street.
2. The mechanic told me the car needed a new water pump; he thought it would cost about $300, including labor.
3. My car isn't worth a lot of money; in fact, it's probably not worth much more than $300.
4. It's a 1995 Nissan Sentra hatchback with about 130,000 miles, but up until last week it had been driving just fine.
5. Over the years I've had good luck with this car, and I've grown quite attached to it.
6. My brother thinks I should get the car repaired, but my sister thinks I'd be foolishly throwing good money after bad.
7. My sister is probably right; still, I'm unhappy about abandoning my car.

8. I could buy my neighbor's 2001 Toyota Corolla, or I could go to the used-car dealer my parents recommended.

9. I'm just not sure it makes sense for me to take out a car loan right now; besides, I don't have any money for a down payment.

10. Maybe I should get the car repaired; then I could buy a new car after I've saved some money over the summer.

Answers to 27-5

POSSIBLE REVISIONS

1. Although she didn't cook when we were very young, she started making cookies, cakes, and some entrees when we were teens.

2. She made us snacks when we got home from school.

3. While she was working as a cook for a summer job, the chef noticed that she had an excellent sense of how long to cook meats and vegetables on the grill.

4. After she finished her shift one night, he offered to give her more training, saying, "You have the potential to be a great cook."

5. Before he said another word, my sister accepted.

6. Since she left that job, she has cooked at many more restaurants and recently finished cooking school.

7. At cooking school, she got a scholarship because she was such a talented student.

8. Even though she likes to have a break from cooking, she is happy to prepare feasts for family holidays.

9. My spoiled family won't consider an event special unless my sister prepares her famous chocolate mousse cake.

10. My sister now works at Chez Henri, where she uses her fabulous cooking skills.

Answers to 27-6

POSSIBLE REVISIONS

1. The TV news recently reported that Jahmal Haney delivered his first baby, even though he was only eight years old.

2. Although Jahmal's mother, Donna Murray, wasn't due for another month, she started having contractions in the middle of the night.

3. Two hours later, she called 911 because she realized she wasn't going to make it to the hospital.

4. When the 911 operator, Sean Stentiford, asked Murray if there was anyone else at home, she handed the phone to her son.

5. After his mother went to lie down in the bedroom, Jahmal listened carefully to Stentiford's instructions.

6. Stentiford told Jahmal to make sure his mother was lying in the middle of the bed since they didn't want the baby to fall on the floor.

7. When Jahmal returned from the bedroom, he told Stentiford he could see the baby's head.

8. Stentiford instructed Jahmal to put his hands under the head as his mother pushed the baby out.

9. Although Jahmal had to run back and forth between his mother in the bedroom and the phone in the living room, he helped deliver his new baby sister, Samantha Elise Murray.

10. The ambulance arrived after the baby had already been born.

Answers to 28-1

POSSIBLE REVISIONS

1. Among college students, halogen lamps have become more popular than traditional incandescent lamps.

2. Halogen lamps are more popular because they are cheaper and brighter.

3. However, there are two problems with halogen lamps: They not only cause fires but also use lots of energy.

4. A 300-watt halogen bulb gets almost three times as hot as a 150-watt incandescent bulb.

5. A Harvard engineering professor discovered that halogen lamps—not toasters, hair dryers, stereos, refrigerators, or computers—were responsible for rising energy consumption in residence halls.

6. Some colleges are considering both banning halogen lamps in dormitories and offering students low-energy fluorescent lamps.

7. The new lamps would be provided either free or at a discount.

8. These energy-efficient lamps cost about four to five times more than halogen lamps.

9. Unfortunately, most consumers would rather save money when buying an item than when using it.

10. To figure out a lamp's lifetime cost, you have to consider the cost of the lamp itself, replacement bulbs, and electricity.

Answers to 28-2

POSSIBLE REVISIONS

1. A migraine is an intense headache characterized by pulsing pain, nausea, dizziness, double vision, and sensitivity to light and sound.

2. Migraines are often triggered by red wine, chocolate, aged cheese, and cured meats.

3. These terrible headaches can also be triggered by certain medicines and food additives.

4. Migraines are three times more common in women than in men.

5. Women's migraines are often hormonal, related to the fluctuation of both estrogen and progesterone during their menstrual cycles.

6. Birth control pills or estrogen replacement therapy can make hormonal migraines much worse.

7. Throughout history, there have been many failed remedies for migraines, such as purging, bleeding, encircling the head with a hangman's noose, and drilling a hole in the skull.

8. In a famous essay entitled "In Bed," the writer Joan Didion argues that people with migraines suffer not only from the headaches themselves but also from the common belief that they are somehow causing their own sickness.

9. Despite what some people think, migraines are caused by neither a bad attitude nor a certain personality trait.

10. An international team of scientists has not only isolated the gene that causes one severe type of migraine but also expects to find genes for more common forms.

Answers to 29-1

POSSIBLE REVISIONS

1. Recently, my friend has had problems concentrating on and finishing the projects she starts.

2. Always very thorough, Karen says she has felt distracted since her brother died of cancer last spring.

3. Sadly, this has gotten in her way at work, where she is expected to complete assignments on time.

4. Fortunately, her boss is very understanding and told Karen that she would like to support her through this difficult time.

5. Recently, Karen went to a psychologist to see if there was anything that Karen could do about her concentration problems.

6. Gently, the psychologist explained that the overwhelming emotions Karen was experiencing were completely normal after the loss of a loved one.

7. "Luckily, these feelings do not last forever," the psychologist explained, "and the grief will eventually become less consuming."

8. Immediately after talking with the psychologist, Karen began to attend a support group for people who have lost relatives to cancer.

9. Amazingly, Karen said she began to feel a little better very soon after joining the group.

10. Determinedly, she is getting back on her feet.

Answers to 29-2

POSSIBLE REVISIONS

1. Typing text messages on her cell phone, my daughter chats with her friends throughout the day.

2. Understanding that I am unfamiliar with this technology, she showed me how it works.
3. Using abbreviated phrases, like "How RU?" in messages, people can send and receive notes quickly.
4. Feeling behind the times when I heard this, I asked my daughter, "Does everyone understand all the abbreviations?"
5. Laughing, my daughter said, "Not all the abbreviations, but you catch on over time."
6. Hoping I would catch on, too, she typed "'Sup" into her cell phone and handed it to me.
7. Watching me closely, she asked, "What do you think that means?"
8. Shaking my head, I said, "I haven't a clue."
9. Throwing her head back, she yelled, "What's up?"
10. Wagging my finger, I replied, not entirely as a joke, "You better not use that kind of language in your English papers."

Answers to 29-3

POSSIBLE REVISIONS

1. Regarded as particularly lucky, the *Essex* was an old whaling ship by the time it sailed its last voyage in 1820.
2. Attacked by a sperm whale, the *Essex* inspired the final scene of Herman Melville's *Moby-Dick*.
3. Passed down over the years through town lore, the larger story actually began after the ship was sunk.
4. Considered enlightened and a good place for free blacks to live during the era of slavery, Nantucket, home of the *Essex*, was a prosperous whaling town.
5. Orphaned and desperate for work, many of the sailors on the *Essex* were only fifteen years old.
6. Determined to record what happened during the attack and in the ninety days

that followed, Thomas Nickerson was a fourteen-year-old cabin boy.
7. Discovered in 1981, Nickerson's narrative recorded starvation, madness, and desperation.
8. Forced to resort to desperate measures to stay alive, twenty of the crew members were stranded on small boats for ninety days after the *Essex* was sunk.
9. Troubled by his captain's obsession, Melville's narrator, Ishmael, ends his story when the boat sinks.
10. Starved and driven to desperate measures, the crew of the *Essex* may have wished for that fate by the end of their ordeal.

Answers to 29-4

POSSIBLE REVISIONS

1. My brother, a paramedic, has some very interesting stories from his work.
2. Rush hour, a tense and hectic time for ambulance workers, afforded him a particularly good story last week.
3. A pregnant woman, a rush hour victim, called from her car phone.
4. The woman started to go into labor, one of the most intense experiences a person can have.
5. The woman, a first-time mother, hoped that an ambulance could rescue her from a traffic jam.
6. Jake, one of the best ambulance drivers in the area, was working with my brother that day.
7. They found the woman, a model of courage despite her pain and fear, about an eighth of a mile down the highway from where she called.
8. They left her car, a 2005 red Lexus, at the side of the road.
9. They lifted her into the ambulance, a godsend to the woman and her unborn child, and sped away.
10. The woman gave birth to her child, a healthy little girl, seven minutes after arriving at the hospital.

Answers to 29-5

POSSIBLE REVISIONS

1. Alice Waters is a well-known chef who has helped bring attention to organic produce and locally grown foods.
2. Waters has a restaurant named Chez Panisse, which is located in Berkeley, California.
3. Chez Panisse uses only locally grown foods that are pesticide- and chemical-free.
4. In recent years, many people who have heard or read about the organic farm movement have become much more aware of the quality of the foods they eat.
5. They have come to realize that the nutritional value of food, which is usually associated only with vitamin content, involves many factors.
6. Organic produce, which often has a higher vitamin content, has to be sold more quickly and is therefore fresher.
7. In addition, organic produce is free of pesticides and chemicals, which can be carcinogenic.
8. Chemicals can have other effects that may be less dangerous but are still undesirable.
9. For example, sulfites, which are often added to fruits and vegetables to prevent discoloration, can produce an allergic reaction in many people.
10. Adding sulfites to fruits and vegetables also makes them appear fresher for longer, which allows fruits and vegetables to be sold several weeks after they have been picked.

Answers to 29-6

POSSIBLE REVISIONS

1. Recently, a group of scientists discovered that babies whose mothers smoked during pregnancy have the same levels of nicotine in their bodies as adult smokers.
2. The results of their study, presented at a meeting of the American College of Cardiology, strongly suggest that these newborns go through withdrawal.
3. Speaking at the conference, Dr. Claude Hanet said that the baby of a smoking mother should be considered an ex-smoker.
4. Conducted by a team of Belgian researchers, the study examined the urine of 273 babies and toddlers.
5. Of these children, 139 were newborns who were one to three days old.
6. Researchers checked the children's urine for cotinine, the substance that remains in the body for several days after nicotine breaks down.
7. Some of the mothers in the study, who had smoked during pregnancy, had newborns with cotinine levels that were about the same as their own.
8. In toddlers with smoking mothers, cotinine levels were significantly higher than in adult nonsmokers who were exposed to secondhand smoke at home.
9. Pregnant women should not only quit smoking but also avoid secondhand smoke, inhaled from other people's cigarettes.
10. Studies have found that even nonsmoking pregnant women who have inhaled secondhand smoke can pass cancer-causing chemicals to their fetuses.

Answers to 30-1

1. The poet laureate is an appointed position.
2. The Library of Congress chooses an American poet to serve annually.
3. Ted Kooser was named poet laureate in 2004, and he is well known for writing poetry while working at a life-insurance company.
4. Have you ever heard of him?
5. Kooser created the "American Life in Poetry" program.
6. It provides a weekly poetry column to newspapers around the country.
7. Newspapers that are interested in poetry can run the column for free.
8. Also, subscribers can read a new poem every week.

9. Each poet laureate has contributed different ideas to the program.
10. To find out more about past poet laureates, visit the Library of Congress Web site.

Answers to 30-2

1. In recent years, you have probably seen many articles written about the healing power of certain foods.
2. Blueberries, for example, contain fiber and vitamin C.
3. Omega-3 fats help in the fight against heart diasese.
4. Salmon and walnuts are two foods that contain them.
5. Heart disease is the number one killer of women in America, but it might become less of a threat if diets are improved.
6. Beans, especially soybeans, might prevent heart disease and some types of cancer.
7. In the Middle East, dates have been praised for thousands of years.
8. Dried fruit, like dates, doe snot require refrigeration and contains many vitamins and minerals.
9. Some people refuse to eat fruit, fish, and nuts because they don't like the taste.
10. However, if you are trying to stay healthy, eating right is essential.

Answers to 31-1

POSSIBLE REVISIONS

1. I wanted to let you know how much I enjoyed meeting you on Monday.
2. Thank you for taking the time to talk with me about the summer internship in the design department of your advertising agency.
3. Nadler & Lattimore seems like an exciting place to work, and the internship sounds ideal for someone with my background.
4. Having taken two courses in graphic design and one in advertising, I think my qualifications meet your requirements.
5. Based on what you told me about the internship, I know that I could do an outstanding job assisting the graphic designers at Nadler & Lattimore.

6. As I mentioned at the interview, this internship represents a tremendous opportunity for me, since I am planning to pursue a career in advertising design after I graduate from college next spring.
7. I have called my references to let them know that you might be contacting them.
8. Please let me know if you have any other questions.
9. I look forward to hearing from you about the internship.
10. Once again, thank you for taking the time to meet with me.

Answers to 32-1

1. advice; write.
2. it's; piece.
3. except; whose; are; than.
4. past; our; right; advise.
5. there; who's; to.
6. used; then; our; their.
7. principle; have; right; your; are; you're.
8. it's; of.
9. conscience; too; who's.
10. know; have; peace; of; quit; to.
11. it's; quite; used.
12. of; and.
13. conscious; new.
14. buy; to; mind.
15. Then; though; knew.
16. to; an; by; two.
17. accept; lose.
18. have; of; affect; and; too.
19. a; than; right; and; your.
20. suppose; find; sit; and.

Answers to 32-2

1. know; who's; advice; you're.
2. used; and.
3. right; our.
4. then; to.
5. twenty-two; through.
6. conscious; effect; by; have.
7. piece.
8. There; accept.
9. quiet; our.
10. lose; knew; mind.

Answers to 33-1

 1. believe.
 2. assuming; hurrying.
 3. Luckily; corrected.
 4. omitted; flipped; *achieve.*
 5. used; worried; submitted.
 6. saying; sloppiness.
 7. portfolios; improvement.
 8. tattoos; laziness.
 9. conceive; encouraging; hopeful.
10. clapped; cheered; speeches.

Answers to 33-2

 1. definitely.
 2. convincing.
 3. preferred.
 4. believe.
 5. troublesome.
 6. cleaner.
 7. happier.
 8. offering.
 9. neighbor's.
10. argument.

Answers to 33-3

 1. stories.
 2. their.
 3. shelters.
 4. making.
 5. scheduled.
 6. hoping.
 7. spotted.
 8. happened.
 9. friendly.
10. admitted.

Answers to 33-4

 1. sophomore.
 2. career; definitely; surprise; friends; a lot; arguments.
 3. incredibly; disappointed; business; jewelry.
 4. probably; secretary; convenience; until; married.
 5. intelligence.
 6. received; encouragement; perceived; athlete.
 7. especially; awful; arithmetic; already; embarrassed; answer.
 8. achieve; meant; succeed.
 9. analyze; interests; environment.
10. weird; excellent.

Answers to 33-5

 1. Until; neither.
 2. tried; describe.
 3. loneliness.
 4. happily; regretted.

 5. disappointed.
 6. necessary; to.
 7. worried; something.
 8. already.
 9. prettiest.
10. immediately; now.

Answers to 34-1

 1. Studies show that newborn babies immediately begin to explore their environment by using their senses of sight, hearing, touch, smell, and taste.
 2. Yet, it is difficult to tell what newborns can perceive because they are often sleeping, dozing, or crying.
 3. **OK.**
 4. They film their eye movements and measure changes in their heart rates, sucking, and sweating.
 5. **OK.**
 6. A newborn sees poorly because its brain, eyes, and nerves have not yet fully developed.
 7. At first, infants can focus only on lines, corners, and the edges of objects.
 8. Patterns with large shapes, clear outlines, and high contrast are what they see best.
 9. Every parent, grandparent, or babysitter knows that infants love to look at people's faces.
10. **OK.**

Answers to 34-2

 1. Some people are more motivated to achieve excellence than other people, so psychologists are interested in understanding why.
 2. People with high achievement motivation have a strong desire to master tasks, and they experience great satisfaction when they achieve success.
 3. In one experiment, researchers gave children a test designed to measure their need for achievement, and then they asked these children to play a ring-toss game.
 4. Those children who had scored low on the test stood so close to the target that they always scored, or they stood so far away that they always missed.

5. In other words, they succeeded at an unchallenging task, or they failed at an impossible one.
6. In contrast, the children who had scored well on the test stood far enough away from the target to make the game challenging, but they did not stand so far away as to guarantee their own failure.
7. Psychologists believe that people with high achievement motivation tend to set challenging but realistic goals for themselves, and they are willing to take risks to achieve those goals.
8. They experience intense satisfaction from success, but they are not discouraged by failure if they feel they have tried their best.
9. People with low achievement motivation also prefer success to failure, but they usually experience relief at *not* having failed rather than pleasure or pride at having succeeded.
10. They do not tend to seek out feedback from critics, nor do they struggle with a problem instead of quitting in the face of failure.

Answers to 34-3

1. According to a recent study, children can unlearn violent behavior in less than six months.
2. Published in *The Journal of the American Medical Association,* the study helps disprove the idea that nothing can be done to stop violence among America's youth.
3. For Americans between the ages of fifteen and twenty-four, violence is one of the leading causes of death.
4. Financed by the Centers for Disease Control and Prevention, the study involved 790 second- and third-graders at twelve schools in the state of Washington.
5. Over a period of sixteen to twenty weeks, about half of these students were taught a violence-prevention curriculum.
6. During the study, the behavior of this group of students was compared with the behavior of the students who did not take the course.

7. Six months after the program ended, students who had taken the course engaged in about thirty fewer aggressive acts per day at school than the students in the other group.
8. Significantly, aggressive behavior (such as hitting, kicking, and shoving) increased in those children who did not take the course.
9. Developed by a Seattle educator, the Second Step antiviolence program consists of weekly or twice-weekly sessions lasting about half an hour each.
10. Widely used in American and Canadian schools, the program is designed to teach empathy, problem-solving, and anger management to preschool through ninth-grade students.

Answers to 34-4

1. Thousands of "snowballs" from outer space are hitting Earth's atmosphere every day, according to scientists at a recent meeting of the American Geophysical Union in Baltimore.
2. Over billions of years, they reported, this bombardment of cosmic slush has added vast amounts of water to Earth's atmosphere and oceans.
3. These extraterrestrial snowballs, made up of ice and cosmic dust, may have played a key role in nurturing life on this planet and perhaps elsewhere in the solar system.
4. They are about forty feet in diameter, the size of a small house.
5. These small, cometlike objects, unlike large comets, are extremely hard to see because they break up into fragments and then vaporize.
6. Astronomers and physicists, however, have speculated about their existence since 1986.
7. Dr. Louis A. Frank, a physicist at the University of Iowa, first theorized about them to explain the dark spots he observed in images of Earth's sunlit atmosphere.
8. Dr. Frank noticed these spots, or atmospheric holes, while analyzing data from NASA's *Dynamics Explorer 1* satellite.

9. NASA's *Polar* satellite, a veteran space explorer, produced more detailed images of these atmospheric holes.
10. Many scientists now believe that these snowballs are hitting Earth's outer atmosphere at an incredible rate of five to thirty a minute, or up to 43,000 a day.

Answers to 34-5

1. Bernard Malamud, who was born in Brooklyn in 1914, wrote novels and short stories about Jewish immigrant life.
2. His parents, who were Russian immigrants, owned a struggling neighborhood grocery store.
3. **OK.**
4. **OK.**
5. *The Natural,* which was made into a movie starring Robert Redford, is considered one of the greatest baseball novels of all time.
6. Malamud's first short-story collection, which won the National Book Award, is called *The Magic Barrel.*
7. **OK.**
8. **OK.**
9. This novel, which is set in Russia, is about a Jewish handyman who is falsely accused of ritual murder.
10. Malamud, who died in 1986, is considered one of the greatest contemporary American fiction writers.

Answers to 34-6

1. Two years ago, my parents decided to sell their house in St. Paul, Minnesota, and retire to Florida.
2. During a vacation they had stopped in Lake Worth, Florida, to visit my father's cousin Lila, and they decided they liked the area.
3. On December 29, 2004, my mother called to tell me that they had put down a deposit on a house that was going to be built in a new development near Lila's condominium.
4. When I heard the news, I said, "Mom, have you and Dad gone out of your minds? Isn't this kind of sudden?"

5. "Yes, it is," she replied, "but I think your father and I have made a wise decision."
6. Both my parents have always insisted that they would never retire to a place like Florida or Phoenix, Arizona, because they enjoy the winter.
7. My father grew up in Madison, Wisconsin, and moved to St. Paul in 1952.
8. **OK.**
9. "Peter, we're putting the Carter Avenue house on the market this May," my mother calmly informed me, "and we expect to be moving to Florida by September or October 2005."
10. On October 3, 2005, my parents moved to a small stucco house at 61 Rosewood Lane, Green Acres, Florida 33463.

Answers to 35-1

1. nation's; schools.
2. students.
3. student's.
4. laws.
5. states; states'.
6. Graham's.
7. Graham's; its.
8. court's; its.
9. Graham's; nation's.
10. Dixon's; her.

Answers to 35-2

1. year's; couldn't.
2. wasn't; students.
3. wouldn't; hour; *A*'s, *B*'s, *C*'s, and *D*'s.
4. hours'.
5. students; *Q*'s, *X*'s, and *Z*'s.
6. it's; year's; we'll; week's.
7. I'm; its.
8. I've.
9. *X*'s; *O*'s; didn't; it's.
10. It's; months'; teacher's.

Answers to 36-1

1. Darryl called his parents from the hospital emergency room to tell them that he had just been in an accident.
2. "I was riding my bike down New Scotland Avenue," he explained when his mother picked up the phone. "A guy who had just parked his van in front of the Bagel Baron opened his door."

3. **OK.**
4. "Luckily, I was wearing a helmet," he said, "or I'd probably be dead."
5. "Are you all right?" interrupted Darryl's mother. "What hospital are you at?"
6. "I hurt my shoulder, but I'm not sure how badly because I haven't seen a doctor yet," replied Darryl. "I'm at St. Peter's."
7. "George," his mother called to his father, "pick up the phone in the kitchen. Darryl hurt his shoulder in a bicycle accident."
8. Darryl said he had to get off the phone because the doctor was ready to examine him.
9. **OK.**
10. "Don't let them do anything to you until we get there and talk to the doctor!" insisted Darryl's father.

Answers to 36-2

1. "I think you would enjoy reading some poems by Martín Espada," my English teacher told me during our conference.
2. "I'm going to lend you a book called *City of Coughing and Dead Radiators,*" she said.
3. "I'll take a look," I replied, "but I really don't like poetry very much."
4. "I had a student last year who announced, 'I hate poetry,' but he changed his mind after reading this book," replied my teacher.
5. A week later I told Professor Macarrulla that I too had changed my mind about poetry after reading Espada's book.
6. "Which poems did you like the best?" Professor Macarrulla asked me.
7. I told her that my favorites were "Borofels" and "Day of the Dead on Wortman Avenue."
8. I explained that "Borofels" reminded me of my own experience growing up in Brooklyn with Puerto Rican parents who spoke very little English.
9. Professor Macarrulla said that her favorite poem in the book was "Who Burns for the Perfection of Paper."
10. "I like that poem," she explained, "because it reminds me that no matter how much success you achieve in life, you should never forget your working-class roots."

Answers to 37-1

POSSIBLE REVISIONS

1. Scientists at Cornell University have discovered something that seems too good to be true: a strain of bacteria that can break down some of the most toxic chemicals in polluted water.
2. Dr. Stephen H. Zinder and his colleagues have found this pollution-fighting organism in sewage sludge (the solid matter produced during sewage treatment).
3. This strain of bacteria breaks down two of the most common pollutants of groundwater: the chemical compounds trichloroethene and tetrachloroethene.
4. Both chlorinated compounds are solvents that are used in such products as glue; paint remover; and cleaning solutions for clothing, machinery, brakes, engines, and electronic parts.
5. These two water-polluting solvents can damage the human nervous system; they are also suspected carcinogens (cancer-causing substances).
6. They are major groundwater pollutants because for years they were handled carelessly—spilled on the ground, poured down drains, and dumped into landfills—before their danger was clearly understood.
7. These solvents seep hundreds of feet into the earth and then dissolve gradually as groundwater—the main source of drinking water for half the U.S. population—flows by.
8. Scientists have known for about fifteen years that bacteria can sometimes change these chlorinated compounds into ethylene (the harmless gas that causes fruit to ripen).
9. However, the exact chemical process—as well as the conditions necessary for it to occur—have been poorly understood until now.
10. The Cornell scientists have figured out that these bacteria break down the solvents by

using them the way people use oxygen: for the cycle of biochemical reactions known as respiration (breathing).

Answers to 37-2

POSSIBLE REVISIONS

1. The 1993 movie *Schindler's List* (directed by Steven Spielberg) won the Academy Award for Best Picture in 1994.
2. The movie tells the true story of an unlikely hero of the Holocaust: a German factory owner from Czechoslovakia who saved thousands of Jews from almost certain death at the hands of the Nazis.
3. This unlikely hero was Oskar Schindler: drinker, gambler, womanizer, and black-market profiteer.
4. The movie features an extraordinary cast: Liam Neeson as Schindler; Ben Kingsley as Itzhak Stern, Schindler's Jewish business adviser and friend; and Ralph Fiennes as Amon Goeth, the brutal and corrupt commander of a slave-labor camp in Nazi-occupied Poland.
5. This Oscar-winning movie was later shown on television without commercial interruption; only a few minutes of the original three-and-a-half-hour film were cut (by Spielberg himself) for the Ford-sponsored broadcast on NBC.
6. The TV broadcast of *Schindler's List* was viewed by sixty-five million people—more than twice the number who saw the big-screen version in movie theaters.
7. Many viewers probably did not realize that the movie was based on a 1982 book (originally published in England as *Schindler's Ark*) by the Australian writer Thomas Keneally.
8. **OK**
9. Keneally's book won England's 1982 Booker Prize for Fiction—the nation's best-known literary award.
10. Keneally's victory generated a huge controversy in England because in the preface the author insists that his book is not a work of fiction; he describes it instead as a "documentary novel" that tells a true story.

Answers to 38-1

1. According to an article in *The New York Times Magazine,* more and more Americans are rejecting their parents' religion.
2. In an article entitled "Choosing My Religion," Stephen J. Dubner analyzes a trend that affects him on a personal level.
3. Dubner, who is an editor at the magazine, grew up in a large Catholic family.
4. His parents, however, both grew up Jewish and converted to Catholicism when they were in their twenties.
5. His mother, Florence Greenglass, and his father, Solomon Dubner, were both born in Brooklyn, the children of Russian and Polish immigrants.
6. When Florence Greenglass was baptized a Roman Catholic, she chose "Veronica" as her baptismal name; Solomon chose the name "Paul."
7. They were married on March 2, 1946, at St. Brigid's Catholic Church in Brooklyn; none of their families attended the wedding.
8. Stephen Dubner, the youngest of eight children, grew up on a farm in upstate New York, near the town of Duanesburg.
9. His family was devoutly Catholic, but by the time Dubner left home for college, he had become uncomfortable with his religion.
10. Under the guidance of his friend Ivan, Dubner began exploring Judaism and learning Hebrew while he was in graduate school.

Answers to 38-2

1. According to Dean Hoge, a sociology professor at Catholic University in Washington, D.C., switching religions is more common in America today than it has ever been in history.
2. In their book *One Nation Under God,* Barry A. Kosmin and Seymour P. Lachman estimate that 30 percent of Americans switch religions or denominations during their lifetimes.

3. Most of these people switch from one Protestant denomination to another, but some changes are more dramatic.

4. Kosmin and Lachman, who surveyed 113,000 people for their book, concluded that the most common reason for switching religions is intermarriage—marrying someone of a different faith.

5. In his *New York Times Magazine* article "Choosing My Religion," Stephen J. Dubner explores his own switch from Catholicism to Judaism, but he also spotlights several other young Americans who have changed religions.

6. Daniel Dunn grew up a Congregationalist but became a Catholic after he almost died in a serious water-skiing accident.

7. Judith Anderson grew up in a Jewish family in Teaneck, New Jersey, but she is now a Buddhist.

8. Like many Jews who practice Buddhism, Anderson has not renounced her Judaism; instead, she feels that she has added another spiritual layer to her life.

9. Fatima Shama is the daughter of a devoutly Catholic Brazilian mother and a Muslim Palestinian father who isn't very religious.

10. She grew up Catholic in the Bronx but began practicing a liberal form of Islam during college.